Sheldon Miller has one previously published book, Stealth Management: With Shared Goals They Will Hardly Know You Are Leading Them. He is a graduate of Lehigh University with a degree in mechanical engineering. Mr. Miller started the Tesco Engineering Company and sold it in 1980, at which time his firm was a major supplier of seismic equipment to the oil industry. He has been issued fourteen patents: one military, one related to golf, the others relating to geophysics. During President Carter's regime he served on a committee that addressed the problem of enhancing creativity in the United States. Mr. Miller is married with three adult children and three grandchildren. He is currently working on his third book.

From
CONCEPT
to CHAOS

OUR CONTEMPORARY CULTURE
IS BEING SADLY NEGLECTED

Sheldon Miller

My thanks:

I have been blessed with a loving family – Rose, Anne, Judy and Steve, Bobby and Bonnie and grandchildren Ellen, Nathan, and Miriam. They have each contributed directly or indirectly to this book which I dedicate to all of them with love.

Contents

Introduction

This book is about many trends that are negatively impacting our culture, some of which are so severe as to almost justify being called terminal. They stem from forces of nature, political mistakes and the misbehavior of society at large. Perhaps the area that we can do the most about has to do with concepts that stem from political actions or inaction that subsequently seem to lead toward chaos. That is why I have chosen the title *From Concept to Chaos*.

The early portion of this book delineates many areas of social disorder in our society. Most of us are already very conscious of some of them, but perhaps this series of essays will give the reader a more comprehensive awareness and a resulting realization of the severity of our problems.

I hope that your study of this book will add to your sense of citizenship and that, if you do not usually vote, it will convince you to do so. More important, when you vote, I hope that you will do so based on your own analysis of the candidates, not because of any sense of obligation or loyalty to party or religious dogma.

Many management books advise corporate executives, "If you want to change your company, you must first change yourself". This is also true of our social and political problems. If we want to improve our society, we must first change ourselves. As Mohandas Gandhi once said, "You must be the change you wish to see in the world". We cannot blame it all on government. The following pages are often sharply critical of government, but be aware that any segment of society, even government, reflects the flaws of society at large. Certainly, there are politicians deserving of criticism for being self-serving and not acting with the best intentions toward their constituents, but we put them in office. This can easily happen when we vote for the party rather than the best candidate or permit our political choices to be single-issue oriented. Businessmen and women who tend to vote for what they believe will be "best for business next year" might be much better off if instead they vote for what will be "best for business over the next several decades". Of course, that requires a greater level of profundity and a high ability to conceptualize.

Many of the topics herein deal with serious problems while others merely refer to annoying flaws in our overall social fabric. However, a large number of them have the potential to ultimately cause chaotic conditions. Some are caused by inappropriate actions by government, but many are unexpected results of the vicissitudes of both man and nature. Those that result from actions by man, often political in nature, usually involve planning that I liken to conceptualization. Even our attempts to beneficially influence or control negative impacts by nature or to improve our many social disorders require such brainstorming or conceptualization. As outlined in topic 34, religion certainly involves conceptualization and is also responsible for much chaos. Thus, the title *From Concept to Chaos* seemed to be both appropriate and likely to arouse concern.

Even most of the topics covered here that do not seem to concern trends toward chaos in the short term do directly or indirectly impact serious trends in the long term. President Obama in his recent address to Congress indicated plans to address many of these problems, but since he has not yet had time to do so as of this writing, they still remain as problems.

Part One
Social Disorder

Section I

Economy of Scale

1. Small is Beautiful

"Small is beautiful" says John Naisbitt, the author of several books that discuss the impact of political, societal, and economic changes that are shaping our future. In a business forum talk several years ago, he pointed out that the number of countries participating in the 1996 Olympic Games in Atlanta would exceed those that were in the previous Olympics by 17 percent, and that number would increase nearly another 50 percent in the games held in the year 2000. He indicated that the world is becoming smaller due to high-tech communications and is much more homogenized as a result. In spite of this influence, there is also a prevalent trend toward increased "tribalism" in which geographically smaller groups of people are willing to fight for their autonomous rights.

The Canadian province of Quebec, which adamantly insists that French is its primary language, has talked of secession. In Western Canada there has also been talk of secession because of the claims that their economic interests are not compatible with those of Eastern Canada, and that economically the government is blatantly partial to Eastern Canada. The breakup of the USSR has resulted in declarations of independence by virtually all of their former provinces. Northern California feels it should not have to share a disproportionately large share of the costs caused by illegal immigration from Mexico. "That's Southern California's problem", they insist. As a result, there has even been agitation to split California into two or more states, a movement that is given little credence by residents of the southern part of the state. In South Africa, the cessation of apartheid caused apprehension that deep dissension would occur between whites and African-Americans. In reality, however, the dissension among differing groups of African-Americans is deeper and more troublesome by far.

These are but a few examples indicating that demographic homogenization does not necessarily work. This trend toward increased tribalism may have a negative long-term effect. It could prevent much of the social and economic benefit that can accrue as a result of diverse peoples uniting in an overall democratic society such as we have enjoyed in the United States.

In business, the world over, the trend also is toward smallness. Large organizations find that they function more efficiently as a decentralized group of small businesses, each permitted to operate autonomously within established guidelines. The downsizing of many conglomerate headquarters from hundreds of employees to but a few employees is another trend toward smallness. Of course, this is done by passing down more decision-making responsibility to the divisions.

Small companies provide a disproportionately large percentage of our innovation and new job creation. In the period from 1963 to 1993, the formation of new companies increased fifteen-fold in the United States, and this trend is being duplicated over most of the world.

"Small is beautiful" seems to prevail for the well-being of people everywhere other than in government, with but a few exceptions. The benefits of smallness could apply especially to government but for the lack of political vision and the inherent resistance to change. Unfortunately, these shortcomings are shared by governments the world over. Investment manager Dr. Mark Mobius, when asked what problems he saw on the international horizon, responded, "The most unsettling problems are political. I'm less concerned about the problems in smaller countries and more worried about the behavior by politicians in popular democratic governments like the United States, Great Britain, Italy, Spain and most others. The politicians in those countries pander to popular tastes and desires in order to be reelected rather than addressing the real economic needs that will affect their country's future". Dr. Mobius, a PhD, manages more than seven billion dollars in foreign investments by various Templeton funds and is based in Hong Kong.

Whether the unit in question is a country, a state, or a business the smallness that results from autonomously managed parts allows the people involved to enjoy a greater sense of participation and commitment. People are then less divisive. It is easier to solve problems and, at the same time, pay heed to individual or regional uniqueness. Proper networking will enable sharing of knowledge, and a headquarters or central governance can provide guidelines as in a well-managed conglomerate. Such guidelines usually include mutually agreed-upon "bottom line" behavior, performance standards, appropriate responses to "breaking the rules", and adequate monitoring. It has been said, "Tell me and I may forget; show me and I may remember; involve me and I will understand". When smallness is accompanied by a sense of involvement, understanding and good team spirit are more likely; discontent is less likely.

The pervasive trend toward smallness is practical only when accompanied by an increase in trust within large organizations. After all, the people who are displaced through downsizing are not the workers at the bottom or the executives at the top. They are predominantly the middle layers of management who are largely responsible for record keeping, monitoring, and quality control efforts, because with the increased level of trust many jobs associated with quality control, record keeping, and monitoring are eliminated. In the "new era" of business, the people at the bottom should be trained to make their own decisions in a team spirit that naturally enhances quality and minimizes the need for monitoring.

If only we could educate political leaders to understand the value of trustworthiness and to develop a team attitude toward the interests of humankind, a very important trend toward smallness could result—a reduction of armaments and the elimination of war between nations. In almost every country, the beneficial economic impact would be huge. Unfortunately, the combined impact of drugs, despots, terrorists, inability to view the "whole problem", and single-issue-oriented international politicians make such idealism most improbable.

This essay on "small is beautiful" seems incongruous when we are surrounded by bigness, especially when virtually all businesses and politicians regard growth as necessary for success. They usually associate growth with increased employment and job stability, an enhanced "bottom line", and even a decrease in crime. Those are pretty positive social benefits, short-term. Unfortunately, they are also capable of producing inflation and a decline in the purchasing value of the dollar. When growth is fostered with but a short-term view and long-term problems are neglected, negative effects may result, as has been the case with our lack of long-term perspective with regard to energy.

There is also much argument as to the validity of the many indices that are used in measuring economic growth. Insofar as these may be in need of change, continuing to rely on them may be harmful. This is because economic indices are based largely on "hard numbers" such as sales, inventories, orders on hand, productivity, freight tonnage, and the like. They do not usually include the value of services and the huge gains that have derived from computer applications (information technology). Worst of all, the politically motivated desire to "look good" to the voters too often results in warping the numbers to make them look better. Such warping, done so surreptitiously as to be totally obscure from the public, can inadvertently contribute to several of the trends toward chaos covered in the following sections.

Perhaps there is need to design a way of inculcating the spirit of smallness into a constructive "politics of scale" that would permit such spirit to permeate our social fabric regardless of how large our society becomes. The sections that follow define many chaotic trends that exist. Topics 35 and 36 suggest how we might respond, using a long-range approach, to improve our performance.

2. Growth May Be Overrated

Cities, states, businesses, churches, and other non-profit organizations constantly strive for growth. It has always been accepted that growth is a necessary ingredient in any formula for success. Perhaps, throughout much of our history and in specific areas of human activity, that claim has had validity. It may still be valid in some cases, but as we continue to deplete the world's natural resources, the time may come when many forms of continued growth will have an increasingly harmful long-range impact on society. Mohandas Gandhi once stated, with great assurance, "Earth provides enough to satisfy every man's need, but not for every man's greed".

In his book *Beyond Growth: the Economics of Sustainable Development,* University of Maryland professor Herman Daly calls the concept of "sustainable growth" an oxymoron. He decries his fellow economists for refusing to acknowledge that a continuing decline of the world's ecological systems will inevitably lead to economic setbacks. He further suggests that economic growth often increases environmental costs more rapidly than it increases production benefits. This, in reality, makes us poorer, not richer. It is his contention that non-renewable natural resources should not be depleted more quickly than permitted by the creation of renewable substitutes. He has a realistic, businesslike concept of the world in which we live and operate with an inventory consisting of natural resources. And, as in the case of a business, we will be in serious trouble if we permit ourselves to run out of inventory.

Although Professor Daly's long-term evaluation of ever-continuing growth has caused him to be poorly regarded by his peers for many years, his thinking is being reevaluated and is now given considerable respect. If Professor Daly's admonitions have validity, our continuing to ignore them has the long-range potential of producing for the world "the ultimate chaos" – namely, the inability of our planet to sustain humankind.

Of course, in regard to controlling our "inventory", we must also be aware of the very serious growth in population, especially within third world countries. China is among the very few countries that recognize this problem.

Section II

Demographic Changes Can Be Demons

3. The Farming Revolution

In 1920, there were over six million farms in the United States. A very large percentage of our population was "on the farm", involved in agriculture-related occupations. Since then, American creativity has resulted in the gradual replacement of most farm workers with mechanized behemoths that can do everything from tilling the soil to picking cotton. Scientists have developed fertilizers that increase crop yields exponentially and chemicals that make them highly resistant to diseases of many kinds. Irrigating systems permit farms to utilize available water more efficiently. Cattle ranches as well as poultry and dairy farms have also been automated to a considerable degree. Today, it is estimated that the number of producing farms is less than six hundred thousand, and the number of people still on the farm may be around three million – a very small portion of our population. The same trend is occurring throughout the world, with the displaced workers migrating to cities. Having visited China on two occasions, my personal observation is that the Chinese government is providing employment to these migrating workers to construct large buildings with only a hoped for need, because many of these buildings remain essentially unused while new ones are being built nearby. A United Nations study in 2007 (*UNFPA State of the World Population*) cites that by the year 2050 over 70 percent of the world's population will live in cities as a result of this continual migration from the farm.

Modernization has permitted America to enjoy the most plentiful food supply in the entire world. Our grocery costs are much less than they would have been had improved farming methods not evolved. In spite of inflation, which has reduced the purchasing power of the dollar to but a fraction of what it was in 1900, feeding ourselves constitutes a much smaller percentage of our cost of living than at that time.

We might conclude that such changes were of fantastic benefit and even "pat ourselves on the back" for having magnanimously shared them with the rest of the world. However, there are other numbers that partially refute such claims.

As we evolved from an agrarian society to an industrial society, millions of unemployed farm workers were forced to migrate to cities. The only new jobs associated with this increase in farming and ranching efficiency were in companies that manufactured chemicals and machinery used by farmers, ranchers, and dairies. They absorbed but a very small percentage of those unemployed farmers. Cities were ill-prepared for such an influx of unemployed people, and many painful social difficulties ensued. Such cities adapted very slowly, if at all, insofar as providing jobs for these former farmers.

As cities have grown, the resulting incursions into wildlife habitats have often caused changes to which animals have been unable to adapt. Recently, for example, in downtown Santa Fe, New Mexico, a 100-pound mountain lion burst through the glass entry door of a jewelry store. Fortunately, after a couple of hours, a state game and fish officer arrived and was able to tranquilize the animal, which was tagged and then released into the wild. I assume that if the same cat were to appear in town again, it might be destroyed with luck, before it attacked people. Such instances of dangerous animals finding their ways into populated areas have been occurring with greater frequency than ever before.

In an article written for *The Times* of London Sir James Goldsmith, the late prominent British industrialist, referred to the urban slums, crime, and welfare problems that proliferate as a result of this migration from the farm to the city. He points out that, over the rest of the world, migration of rural populations continues and will probably reach another two billion people over the next decade or two. As in the United States, these people will have been uprooted from their normal culture and will be ill-prepared for a new vocation. Many will live in urban slums for a period and will require charity or government entitlements of various kinds. In addition, such "social unrest" certainly contributes to increased crime and potential divisiveness among political parties, ethnic groups, and economic strata.

Professor Walter Williams of George Mason University has noted that the cost of poverty programs in the United States since 1960 exceeds the sum of the assets of the 500 largest companies in America plus the estimated value of all United States farmland. He then adds that the expenditure of large sums of money, although well intended, has not solved such problems. They remain and are becoming worse. These poverty programs are true examples of concepts leading to chaos.

In-as-much as we all agree that no one should suffer from hunger or unduly from the elements, it is easy to conclude that mechanized farming has helped to reduce world hunger, and has, in that regard, been a boon to society. However, the many side effects have taken a very negative toll on our physical, social, and economic well-being. Yes, such a statement is too simplistic, and there are many other factors involved, including tremendous growth in population. There is truth, however, in the observation that most of the ills resulting from our change from an agrarian society to an industrial one could have been ameliorated with proper planning. Now that we are changing from an industrial society to one that is information-based, we probably will suffer again from lack of planning.

Yes, our food supply is plentiful, and the shelves we see in our supermarkets are full, attractive, and colorful. However, people who can remember back seventy-five or more years ago commonly agree that tomatoes, beets, green beans, and many other farm products do not have the superior natural taste they had before the farming revolution. Chemicals, poor soil conditioning, and early harvesting all have contributed to degrading their taste and, some say, to a decrease in nutritional value. In turn, eating habits, especially of our children, have been more easily altered toward less healthy foods. This change in our eating habits, in all likelihood, would have been more difficult for those who influence us through advertising had the good natural taste of foods remained.

Foods available to us seventy-five years ago contained less saturated fat and were therefore healthier. Today, only if you go into a fine restaurant will you (sometimes) find the menu bragging that they are serving "free-range" chicken as opposed to the mass produced "hothouse" type of chicken commonly available to us. The free-range chickens are raised as chickens were before the farming revolution and are not only better tasting but are considered healthier to eat as well.

The changes in taste and nutritional quality of our foods have, undoubtedly, contributed to many health problems and to today's huge cost of medicine. What the tradeoff of these negatives is against the lower-cost availability of foods is difficult to evaluate, but the huge sums of money spent on natural foods, vitamins, and food supplements at health food stores by those who can afford them provide testimony that a large percentage of our population is concerned about our food quality but can do little about it.

We often see reports, such as the 2004 report in *The Internet Journal of Urology*, that cite a steady decrease in human sperm count and sperm quality in western industrialized countries. There seems to be a huge increase in Alzheimer's disease, diabetes, allergies, cancer, mental illness, ulcers, and learning disabilities over the past fifty years. Yes, these statements are subject to much argument, especially in the face of increased longevity. It certainly is true that many of these ills were unrecognized and often unreported years ago, but the fact that so many older people agree that they seem more prevalent now gives that assumption considerable credence. The increase is not entirely due to more accurate record keeping. To the degree that they are true, could our tampering with nature be partially to blame? Not subject to argument is the fact that large numbers of people have improved their overall health through reduced consumption of those foods that have been directly or indirectly tampered with through the use of chemicals and drugs.

Those in drug and chemical businesses can be proud of many good influences such as the virtual elimination of polio, chicken pox, and scarlet fever, and the reduced death rate from many others diseases. Certainly, antibiotics have prevented many deaths. These examples of medical progress, plus greatly improved sanitation, have contributed to an increase in our lifespan. To these claims should be added, however, that antibiotics are becoming less effective as many types of bacteria develop resistance to them. This is particularly true of many species of bacteria found in hospitals. Such antibiotic-resistant bacteria are referred to as super germs.

To dwell so heavily on the long-term effects of farm chemicals, drugs used in the feeding of farm animals, and the ascent of curative medicine over preventive medicine will be severely criticized by many. To include such data is important, however, since present trends in the cost of medical care may very well produce chaotic conditions if left unchecked. A few medical schools, including the University of Arizona, have added courses in preventive medicine. The benefits to be gained could have a significant effect on the manner in which government is trying to get a "handle" on the cost of medicine. This potential good cannot happen, however, if our politicians continue to be led by lobbyists of the drug industry whose prime consideration is financial profit.

4. Immigration and Ethnic Problems

Throughout most of our history, the United States has welcomed immigrants from a wide variety of cultures. Except for the period during Hitler's reign in which an entire boatload of German refugees was turned away by President Roosevelt, there seemed to be a limited "open door" for those who might suffer persecution, or worse, if prevented from leaving their homeland. Many were permitted to come to the United States only if they had a sponsor so as not to become a burden upon our society. Even with that requirement, thousands of foreigners began migrating to our shores beginning in the latter part of the nineteenth century. The migration was largely controlled as it flowed through Ellis Island, and most immigrants had someone to depend on while learning to accommodate to America and its mores. Predominantly, they settled in our large cities, where they were welcomed as a source of cheap labor.

Although our government has placed varying numerical limits on immigration through the years, the numbers of immigrants in some of our larger cities amplified the effects of those migrating from the farm. Today, the number of immigrants in some of our cities is so high as to make any long-term effects of urban migration from the farm small by comparison.

Today, we no longer have an Ellis Island funnel for all immigration. Since that time, the level of immigration has significantly increased with a growing percentage of those arriving illegally. The benefit of an immigrant having a sponsor has long since been forgotten. Our West Coast has untold numbers of people who have entered the United States illegally, largely from Mexico, seeking financial security. They usually find a way around the law requiring a Green Card to be legally employable and soon are working for minimum wage. Sometimes, they are employed illegally for less than minimum wage. Often, such people acquire a social security card and thereby become potential recipients of the many forms of social entitlements available to those whose income is beneath what is defined as poverty level. So far, efforts by our immigration service to stem the flow of aliens across the Mexican border have been so minimal as to be ineffective. The resulting cost burden contributes to our negative national budget.

The large number of immigrants entering from the Far East, added to the foreign population already in our midst and the continuing influx from Mexico, may ultimately give us a population majority of first and second generation foreigners.

Our permissive attitude in allowing such massive migration would be a fine example for the rest of the world were it managed so that its effect was not, in a major way, contributing to the decay of our social fabric. This is in spite of the fact that many immigrants not only accommodate rapidly but also become prominent contributors of talent.

What until now has been an immigration policy with good intent can become another contributor to chaos. To eliminate it would be contrary to one historical part of our mission, to be a haven of freedom. We must, therefore, find a good way to limit it, a way that would be pragmatic and yet free of prejudice. In 2007 Congress refused to grant amnesty to the millions of illegal immigrants from Mexico, and it appears unlikely to address the situation in the near future. When the economy is strong, immigration is high and when the economy is bad immigration is low. This pattern prompts some to say that immigration problems solve themselves.

Ethnic problems do not exist in nearly ethnically homogeneous nations such as Japan. In the United States and Great Britain, due to appreciable immigration, there is great cultural diversity and many ethnic problems result. Because, in our case, the Founding Fathers did not contemplate such a situation, our laws are constantly being revised, after the fact, and usually as a result of legal interpretation that follows litigation.

When we must debate whether or not English should be declared the language of our land, our ethnic problems have gotten way beyond "out of hand" and are bordering on chaotic. With foreigners arriving in our country faster than we are able to integrate them into our society, we are suffering from "uncontrolled invasion" according to James Goldsmith in his book *The Trap*.

Many immigrants fail to become part of our society. They continue to communicate primarily in their native tongues and depend on others of the same background for their social lives. This insularity amounts almost to a type of tribalism. It is not until the next generation, assuming they go to school here as young children, that there is significant accommodation to our mores. This suggests that, although there are exceptions, the time required to integrate immigrants into our society can be as long as a generation (twenty-five to thirty years). If so, it is easy to understand that unless the rate of integration is adequately controlled, we could cease to be a nation with the degree of cohesiveness envisioned by our founders. The idea of the United States being a melting pot for freedom seekers immigrating from all over the world will not work. It worked better when the majority of immigrants were from Europe, because their culture was similar to ours. That is not so with most immigrants from non-European countries.

It should be noted that there are tribal-like groups such as the Amish in multiple areas of our country who do not assimilate. That they do not do so is probably due to their being largely agrarian - not only because of their religious beliefs. Most of the other ethnic and immigration considerations discussed in this section concern people who become part of our "industrial society".

The culture of a people cannot be changed quickly; it must evolve over a long period of time. The many republics of the USSR now fighting for their independence did not lose their ethnic uniqueness under decades of communist control. The Shah of Iran failed to modernize his people because their ingrained life patterns could not change so rapidly. Examples such as these can be chosen from every continent. You cannot change culture by edict. If we who think of ourselves as "good ole Americans" become outnumbered by immigrants before they have integrated into our culture, we may find it necessary to change appreciably to accommodate to their cultures. For example, business telephones often answer a call with the question "English or Spanish" and in driver exams written information is often printed in both English and Spanish. Instructions for assembling and trouble shooting appliances often are duplicated in other languages.

It is easy to conclude that we in the Western world do not know how to deal well with diversity. Our usual approach is to push those from other cultures to be like us. However, it is impossible to legislate social homogenization. It can only be a slow, almost evolutionary process. This may sound facetious, but be reminded that "with homogenization the cream no longer comes to the top".

During most of 2008, in which the United States has suffered from both inflation and economic woes, not only has immigration from Mexico diminished appreciably but many Mexicans living in the United States have decided to return to Mexico. The large amount of funds being sent back to families back home (in Mexico) by Mexicans in the United States has also decreased considerably. These observations are used by people who claim that illegal immigration is not a problem because economics and job availability will automatically control it.

Sociological Change
Can Produce Social Angina

Introduction

The facets of sociological change are so numerous that only some of the prominent ones are discussed in this section. Within those that are addressed by government, attempts are being made to influence change, but for the most part, such attempts are ineffectual with regard to long-term benefit. Chaotic influences seem to be winning the race. Although this is very evident, statistically, our government cannot decide how deeply to be involved. This seems true the world over.

When government endeavors to alleviate the misfortunes within segments of society that result from economic or social imbalance, its effort usually takes the form of an entitlement. Sometimes its actions are 100 percent political, such as in the case of the millions spent to support tobacco growers, even though tobacco is universally regarded as a harmful and addictive product. It certainly was an oxymoron to subsidize the farming of tobacco, and then, through our many entitlement programs and Medicare, pay billions of dollars in medical care for illnesses that derive from or are aggravated by smoking. Fortunately, that practice was discontinued in 2004.

Government also concerns itself with the support and regulation of many activities which it deems, need federal control rather than being left to the control of the states. Certainly it is true that, left to the states, education might soon vary in quality, and students in some areas of the country would have a marked advantage over those from school systems that were inferior by comparison. It could cause problems for those seeking entrance to colleges or looking for employment in another area of the country. Long-term, however, would such inequities largely disappear as a result of competition, or would regional provincialism dominate? Such considerations are continually debated in the halls of Congress, in national magazines, and in our local newspapers.

In August of 1995, Senator Bill Bradley announced he would not seek re-election to the Senate when his term of office expired two years hence. Among his reasons for that decision was "that on a basic level, politics is broken". He pointed out that neither party represented his political views and that both had moved away from the mainstream voter. Because Senator Bradley is regarded with deep respect for his intellect, integrity, and energy, his departure left a void that has been difficult to fill. Senator Bradley's decision followed the departures of other highly qualified but frustrated legislators such as former senators David Boren and Sam Nunn. When people of such ability leave government service, not only do we suffer a continuation of "broken politics", but the collective ability of our Congress to improve things is diminished.

Fordham University's Institute for Innovation in Social Health has been issuing an Index of Social Health since 1985. Using statistics that go back over twenty-five years, they produce indicators of how well our society is doing in sixteen areas which include infant mortality, unemployment, drug abuse, crime, affordable housing, and the gap between rich and poor. They have noted a startling decay in our "social health", prompting them to state, "The quality of life has come unhinged from our economic growth". An article in a May 25th, 2007 issue of *The Wall Street Journal* states, "A study by several prominent think tanks indicates the typical American family's income has lagged far behind productivity growth since 2000, a departure from most of the post World War II period. The up escalator that has historically ensured that each generation would do better than the last may not be working very well". The title of that article is, "Men in Their 30s Lag behind Their Fathers in Pay". It further states that between 1947 and 2000, productivity rose 56 percent while family income rose 29 percent. Between 2000 and 2005, productivity rose 16 percent while median income fell 2 percent challenging "the notion that a rising tide will lift all boats".

With the cost of government spiraling out of control, federal government entitlements should be reviewed individually, prompting such questions as:

- Is it necessary?
- Can it be done better at the state level?
- Can it be made more effective?
- Can it be more rehabilitating in effect rather than creating dependency?

A review of some of our social problems follows.

5. Government Entitlements

Housing

A well-intended public housing project often becomes a boarded-up, fenced-in and locked, unoccupied eyesore with broken windows and ugly graffiti a few years later. Sharon Cohen, an Associated Press writer, in an article published in the LA Times in July 1995, quotes a resident of a large public housing project managed by the Chicago Housing Authority. "Sue Sago's first days in public housing began with an omen: with the elevators broken, she had a heart-thumping climb up and down 11 flights of dark, urine-soaked stairs, towing her children, groceries and laundry. She shivered when the heat didn't work; stuffed clothes under her door to prevent flooding from the spewing burst water pipes outside, and often feared stray gunfire would hit her kids". Sue Sago's public housing experience is about as bad as it gets, but none of her complaints are unusual. Recently, the housing complex in which she lived has been taken over by the Department of Housing and Urban Development, a federal agency.

Even though the federal government has taken over and their investigation has uncovered gross wrong doing and financial scandal in prior management of that complex, Sue Sago remains skeptical that the new management will truly correct things. She certainly is justified in her pessimism, since projects that have been managed by agencies of the federal government often have been fraught with such problems, albeit to a much lesser degree.

Certainly, the failure of many public housing projects can be blamed squarely on the poor value systems of the inhabitants, but that is no excuse. People who would otherwise suffer from lack of housing cannot be left out in the cold, and the concept of low-cost public housing is not necessarily wrong. However, for publicly supported high-rise housing to cost much more per domicile than an individual home is without justification. To plan such monstrous projects without soliciting input from the tenants-to-be is gross dereliction in the planning process. To install management for a public housing project that does not encourage in-depth participation, including volunteer time, by the residents predisposes it to chaotic decay. It has been clearly demonstrated that if tenants-to-be have influence in the design and decor of a housing project they will have interest in keeping it looking nice. They sometimes organize a tenants' "governance committee" to oversee compliance to rules they collectively establish.

One of the finest efforts to provide housing for those suffering financial difficulties is the program called "Habitat for Humanity", which has become international in scope and has had avid support from former President Carter. Unfortunately, the Habitat for Humanity program is not large enough to eliminate the need for other public housing projects.

Health Care

Shortly after his inauguration, President Clinton appointed his wife to head a commission to design a proposed revision to our welfare system that would provide medical care to everyone in our country from cradle to grave. In advancing such a sweeping change, Mrs. Clinton and her advisors proposed funding the program though revisions in the tax code and appreciable reductions in medical costs through controls on drug and hospital pricing. This considerable and sincere effort by Mrs. Clinton's task force was wasted, because Congress was able to find many flaws in it, and perhaps the public was not ready for change. Some of the flaws were excessively optimistic assumptions, and others were blatant errors. There also was considerable lobbying for retaining the old methods.

Apparently, no other country has a national healthcare system worthy of emulating in its entirety, although the system in France seems superior to most others. Therefore, a national healthcare program has little near-term likelihood of enactment in the United States as of this writing. The need for such a program still exists, evidenced by the considerable number of people, especially those below the poverty line, who are inadequately served by our present medical system. It should be noted that virtually every country in the Western world, other than the United States, has a national healthcare system that is available to all of its people without distinction.

Health systems in Canada and in England attempt to control costs by keeping many charges at very low levels. The result is an unsatisfying livelihood for some who work in the field of medicine. Another cost-lowering influence in both countries is their focus on primary care providers. This is usually less costly than depending heavily on emergency-room or specialty care as is the case in the United

States. Often, medical attention requires the patient to be on an appointment list for several months, making the treatment less effective than prompt attention could provide. Those who can afford to seek medical attention outside the confines of National Healthcare often do so at their own expense or through private insurance plans. Such attention costs considerably more than that provided by the system and sometimes is satisfied best by traveling to another country, an option exercised constantly by Canadians who travel to the United States for medical services.

In the United States, for-profit Health Maintenance Organizations (HMO's) are growing rapidly, largely because of the pressure of insurance companies to control costs. HMO's do reduce medical costs by putting all personnel on salary and implementing policies that reduce the prevalence of what they consider unnecessary, expensive testing. They also limit the charges by physicians for which full reimbursement will be allowed. They occasionally force reductions in the price of drugs by pressure tactics applied to drug companies. Hospitals are competing for their patient share by employing salaried physicians and severely reducing costs; attention given a hospital patient is much less apt to be performed by a registered nurse; the level of sanitation often suffers, and errors are more apt to occur. As in the case of automobiles, competition may correct these problems over a long time, but should medical quality be compromised for such a long period?

Many doctors who have been in practice for many years long for the good old days when regard for the patient was more personal, and failure to collect 30 to 40 percent of the fees due him or her was considered normal. He or she was still able to earn a good living. At that time it was not necessary to discharge a patient from the hospital earlier than seemed prudent merely because of the insurance company's insistence. Medical ethics did not have to be compromised because of imposed rules. A procedure that was other than the norm could be invoiced based on the time involved rather than the charge assigned by an insurance company that might be considerably lower or higher. Adequate and well-trained staff aided in the practice of top quality medicine rather than merely monitoring what once could be reliably delegated. In "the good old days", a few doctors may have been guilty of greed to some degree, but now the insurance companies, the hospitals, and HMOs also are guilty of greed – with the HMOs offering their top executives huge salaries. Of course, to be fair, even then there were those few who found it difficult to obtain adequate medical attention.

An NBC broadcast of the television program Dateline a few years ago presented the case of a nursing home patient being charged $45 each for each medical gauze compress (they appeared to be four to five inches square), an item available in most drugstores for considerably less than a dollar when bought a few at a time. The man's son tried hard, but without success, to have that bit of malfeasance corrected. The program concluded that such fraud was costing our Medicare program over $46 million per day, and no one in authority seemed to want to do anything about it. It certainly makes one wonder what sort of pressure is being brought to bear that prevents Congress from correcting such problems. A doctor friend of mine has related instances of doctors being paid nearly $100 to read the printout of a scan that required less than ten minutes. The doctor makes out like a burglar in such an instance, but can easily rationalize accepting such payments because Medicare or other insurance coverage may allow only a paltry thirty dollars for an initial patient visit, which typically does not even cover office overhead. Such mismanagement, although indefensible, is prevalent in our Medicare system and probably will continue. Hospitals routinely need to compensate for what they lose on bed charges by relying on other modes of reimbursement for which they are overcompensated. Many medical practitioners will agree hospital and physician reimbursements often are not based on anything rational.

In the field of medicine, government intervention has created near chaos. The cost of insuring doctors from lost revenue due to patients' failure to pay their bills might be considerably less than Medicare and might also vastly improve availability of good medical treatment, even to the indigent. This is a rather provocative statement and certainly is not based on much study. I do wish to point out; however, that even benevolent government involvement too often is without sufficient planning. Government has created a program for people who are unable to afford conventional access to medical care. This is referred to as Medicaid. When people can show total net worth not exceeding seven to eight thousand dollars, they can qualify for Medicaid. Medicaid pays the doctor at a lower rate than other types of insurance coverage. For this reason, an increasing percentage of doctors are refusing to accept Medicaid patients. Medicaid coverage varies considerably from state to state, and certainly being needy does not qualify you to benefit from Medicaid until your net worth becomes low enough.

Alternative medicine has many variations, including chiropractic, acupuncture, kinesiology, naturopathy, reflexology and vitamin therapy. Doctors are influenced by drug companies to have low regard for alternative medicine even though there are very many instances of people being helped by alternative medical approaches after experiencing little or no help from orthodox medical approaches. There is an almost religious admonition from drug companies for medical doctors to strongly advise against the use of any drug or supplement that has not been double-blind tested. In double-blind testing, a significant number of people are treated with a drug; their results are compared to those of a like number of people treated with a placebo. Neither the experimenters nor the subjects know which group is receiving the real drug and which the placebo. Hence the test results are presumed to be unerringly accurate. Unfortunately, history has shown that even such testing, presumed to be without bias, can be inaccurate by accident, or even intent, if the wrong type of people are chosen for the test or the dosage level is not ideal. Because double-blind studies are very expensive, the financially smaller companies cannot afford such studies.

Natural supplements are not profit producers for large drug companies and are therefore available only from other sources. The fact that they have helped large numbers of people is largely overlooked by the orthodox medical community, and thereby the public is often ill-served and sources for medical cost reduction overlooked.

In spite of the foregoing negative comments about double-blind testing, it is a very valuable tool in regulating and approving drugs when properly applied without bias, and drug companies cannot be faulted for their attention to the bottom line. It is too bad, however, that they do not direct, at least some of their corporate strength toward exploring the potentially beneficial uses of vitamins and food supplements.

During the Second World War, there was the case of a chiropractor drafted into the army without recognition of his expertise. His army company buddies became aware of his training and would sometimes ask for his help. This resulted in his company accounting for significantly fewer visits to sick bay, triggering an investigation for the reason. After the investigators found out that he had been treating fellow soldiers, he was ordered to cease doing so. Soon the company's sick bay dependence returned to normal. The benefit of chiropractic medicine has caused it to become very popular throughout the United States, Canada, and Europe, but it is the rare physician who would consider recommending it to a patient. The same story applies to most other alternative forms of medicine. But for unjustified resistance, they could serve to improve our health and save much medical expense.

Finally, as of this writing, there does seem to be a small trend toward liberalism, and a few medical schools are beginning to include alternative medical approaches. Even orthopedists occasionally recognize chiropractic medicine to be helpful in diagnosing problems that do not show up on x-rays. Insurance companies are also beginning to approve limited payment of claims from chiropractors.

The late Peter Drucker, a highly respected advisor to industry, said a few years ago that the United States could no longer claim the best medical school in the world. That distinction belonged to New Delhi, India. He did not say why that was so. However, many of our United States medical schools, such as Vanderbilt, are now exploiting technologies that allow disease modeling in an effort to improve the abilities of their students. With disease modeling, a computerized mannequin programmed to simulate ailments and response to treatment is used as a teaching tool and has proven to be of significant help. Some medical schools are also slowly beginning to include alternative medical knowledge which expands the scope of available responses to health problems.

In his recent documentary *Sicko,* Michael Moore declared that significant statistics indicate that the state of our health and the quality of our healthcare system are in serious need of improvement. His many detractors pooh-pooh his documentary as biased, exaggerated, and inaccurate. Perhaps his detractors can find a few legitimate flaws in the documentary, but the basic precepts seem very valid. If Moore sincerely wants to make an impression with it, it follows that he must use some of the exaggeration techniques proven effective by the advertising profession. He seems "right on" in saying we can learn much by studying the positive attributes of the many health systems of foreign countries.

A study by *Business Week* ,in their June 22nd 2007 issue, compared patient waiting times and found that only 47 percent of United States patients could get a same-day or next-day appointment. This was a worse situation than in every other country studied except Canada. Michael Moore's assertion that our drug companies purchase too much political influence in the interest of fattening their profits through large political contributions is certainly true. His reference to life expectancy in the United States no longer being exemplary is borne out by a study reported in the September 2006 issue of PLoS Medicine (a Peer Reviewed Open Access Journal). In that study, Dr. Christopher Murray, head of the Institute for Health Metrics and Evaluation at the University of Washington demonstrated that life expectancy in the United States is exceeded by one-fifth of all other countries. (In my discussion with a highly respected physician I was told that that such statistics in the United States are not caused by bad medicine but instead by our lifestyle). The study found that residents of forty countries, including Cuba, Taiwan and most of Europe, had life expectancies better than ours even though considerable improvement has been made here over the last few generations. We are nineteenth in infant mortality, although this may be largely caused by mothers-to-be not receiving timely medical care.

In a January 10th, 2008 issue of the *Economist,* an article entitled *Where Have All The Dollars Gone?* stated that "America lags behind its peers in preventing avoidable deaths". The Economist cites research by Ellen Nolte and Martin Mckee at the London School of Hygiene and Tropical Medicine that looked at deaths which should have been preventable by proper health care in people under the age of seventy-five for the five-year period ending in 2003. These included deaths resulting from bacterial infections, treatable cancers, diabetes and surgical complications; over a fifth of male deaths and nearly a third of female deaths resulted from such causes. They found that where most countries cut "amenable mortality" rates on the average 16% from 1997 to 2003. The United States cut "amenable" deaths by only 4% during the same period. It was at the bottom of the table. Nolte and McKee highlighted the significance of their findings by saying that raising our performance to the level of the average rich country could prevent 75,000 "excess" deaths per year. By matching the top three countries surveyed, we could save 100,000 lives per year. The article did say, in America's defense, that it does have an impressive history of medical innovation, but our huge spending on health leaves sobering gaps in progress.

The article is at fault for not comparing "apples to apples". Had their statistics for all countries included only those who have access to health care they would have arrived at different conclusions. Those, in our country, not receiving adequate health care include too many people on drugs, too many people not receiving prenatal care, a large number of social misfits, and many who should be but aren't receiving treatment for mental illness. These cases considerably warp our life-expectancy data and reflect unfairly on our medical profession.

Health insurance premiums have risen to a point at which many employers, who have traditionally borne most of the cost of such insurance, if not all of it, are now finding it beyond their financial ability to do so. Health insurance premiums have risen 78 percent since 2001 according to the Kaiser Family Foundation as reported by the Washington Post in their issue of March 24th, 2008. They report that the average family plan offered by a company now costs $12,106. Companies pay an average of $8,824 for such coverage, with the worker paying the rest. Obviously, something needs to be done to alleviate this problem.

It has long been recognized that children's medical care is different from adult medicine. This is the reason for the specialty of pediatrics. Today, senior citizens comprise such a large percentage of our population that there is probable justification for an equally recognized specialty in geriatrics. The ailments of older people are certainly different, and they seem to be more chronic in nature. One older acquaintance of mine refers to his annoying medical problems as a disease called "I-IOTIA", which, with a bit of poetic license, is an acronym for "If it isn't one thing it's another". He claims it is more prevalent than arthritis.

Food Stamps

The government's purpose in supplying food stamps to those in severe financial need is to prevent malnutrition, particularly with regard to children. As now implemented that program is so severely flawed as to almost defy imagination. As we so frequently read, food stamps are sometimes sold for money used to buy drugs, are used by people who drive expensive cars to the grocery store to make their purchases, and too often are traded for foods that are known to contribute to ill health. When the program permits the indigent to purchase unhealthy foods, it inadvertently contributes to malnutrition. These are but a few examples of the program's flaws. Recipients of this program have been able to find so many ways to misuse it that the government's ability to monitor it has become hopeless.

Because most of the program's participants probably are needy and endeavor to use their food stamps as intended, it is too bad that the poor ethics of the minority are ruining a program that has such good intentions.

During the Great Depression of the 1930s, soup kitchens were established by churches and many other types of nonprofit organizations. The high percentage of unemployed people made the need for food supplementation even more serious than it is today. That method of getting food to those in need had virtually no elements of fraud or misuse, but there were disadvantages. It was more demeaning in that those who came to eat had to attend public eating halls. The food was often unpalatable because there was little effort to make it enjoyable, and such "soup kitchens" were not convenient to those who did not live in the cities.

As ways are sought to severely reduce the cost of government and balance our national budget, programs such as food stamps may suffer extinction which may result in hunger, illness, and even death for many. If, instead, a way were found to redesign the program and make it more efficient, much money could be saved. Today, unlike the 1930s, we have the United Way program in virtually all cities. Their local boards of directors are made up of volunteers who are regarded as leaders in their communities with an abiding interest in serving those in need in many areas of social welfare. In conjunction with the United Way, local civic and religious leaders would likely be able to redesign the food stamp program to make it perform more effectively. Although United Way is only a fund raising activity on behalf of the many nonprofit organizations belonging to it, it does monitor those organizations to assure that each spends the allotted money effectively.

With food stamps, it may be necessary to replace profit-making participants such as grocery stores as redeemers of food stamps, and establish a different type of nonprofit food distribution. A United Way agency might then be the recipient of federal food stamp allotments and operate the program locally with monitoring by United Way. There are, no doubt, many other possible solutions.

In the July 21st 1997 issue of Time Magazine, Elaine Rivera of Newport News reported that, in many areas of the country, the demand for emergency food has shot up markedly. Government, she reported, was providing 3.4 percent of publicly distributed food, compared to 22.2 percent in 1991. The decline was due to the decision by our Congress to reduce the federal food stamp program and depend more on local charity. Analysis proves that indigent unemployed are not the only people who depend on supplemental food. To a larger extent than realized, the working poor – those who have jobs and are trying to be self-supporting but are unable to generate a living wage rely on it as well. Rivera's observations are true even today.

As corporate America has undergone restructuring, corporate CEOs have justified personal financial rewards that seem unconscionably large and the class of employees who make up our working poor has failed to share in our so-called "prosperity". We have an urgent need to address this situation. Were we to suffer another serious depression, those people in need could become a threat to our entire social structure, including the potential for insurrection.

Education

Our government involves itself in education in many ways, all of them constant subjects of debate between those who want children educated "their way" and those who believe that education should be broadly preparatory for the challenges life has to offer. "Their way" often prefers to: (1) deny the evolution of humankind, (2) assure that curricula include the practice of religion, (3) eliminate or modify undesirable elements of history, and (4) prevent the use of "classically accepted" and important books because they are in conflict with provincial attitudes. Parents who desire "their way" education for their children are, in effect, saying, "I do not trust my children to come to sensible conclusions on their own after they reach maturity; I must inculcate them now with my positively correct attitudes". Judy Estrin in her book *Closing the Innovation Gap* documents the decline of creativity in the United States in the past twenty years. This increasing fear of our children growing up thinking for themselves and perhaps not conforming to our attitudes is a very large contributor to our decline in innovation. She points out how the rest of the world is passing us by. We no longer evidence the type of creative seed planting that, twenty to thirty years later, produces the scientific creativity that permitted us to be first on the moon or to place the Hubble telescope in orbit to permit exotic exploration of space. Such innovation originates from basic research that is becoming somewhat rare in the United States because it takes years for it to pay off economically, if at all.

The highly regarded psychologist Abraham Maslow (now deceased) coined the expression "self-actualized person" to describe the type of individual best equipped to take advantage of his or her inherent abilities. Most people fail to achieve such status. If politicians would accept the precept that the mission of public education should be to equip our youth to take fullest advantage of their innate abilities, they would influence education with that mission in mind and would not be influenced by prejudiced voting groups.

It is important that educational opportunity be equal for all, and that schools in non-white areas not be inferior. Legislating school integration was intended to eliminate inferior schools. Instead, it has caused the cost of education to rise far beyond the value of any measurable benefit, and contributed to lower academic achievement. It has also resulted in almost uncontrollable behavioral problems and an appreciable migration of students to private schools. As is so common when government steps in, the planning was short-term-oriented. It did not provide for trial evaluation. More importantly, it was incomplete in that it failed to recognize that in six hours of school per day, you cannot overcome any contrary or less than positive influence suffered by the student during the other eighteen hours of the day which would be true for any student regardless of background. It often would be desirable to educate parents so that they are better able to aid in their children's education. It also failed to address the possibility that a planned gradual integration of schools might be more practical. Certainly, a long-range goal of properly integrated schools would be ideal. There may be no better way of integrating schools than letting that goal result from integrating housing, a process that is gradually occurring throughout the country.

In June of 2007, our Supreme Court struck down voluntary school desegregation in Louisville, Kentucky and in Seattle, Washington saying that practice is not free of racial prejudice in that it was conceived to apply primarily to African Americans. Schools now contemplate accomplishing the same goals by establishing "diversity via income" which inherently would not apply only to minorities. How the Supreme Court may interpret the legality of such an approach remains to be seen, but again, such a change may not work, even if left unchallenged by the Court, if educational authorities fail to use a participative approach. That would require input from all segments of society that would be affected.

Two students, having equal learning ability, may progress at entirely different speeds if one is getting parental reinforcement and support and the other is not. This is one of our most pervasive problems, and it is not being properly addressed. Many parents who do not meaningfully aid their children with their schooling mean well but are ill prepared to do so. They do not deserve criticism; they need education as much as their children do. Aiding such parents should be an important component of any attempt to improve education, an admonition that I am guilty of repeating, but it deserves repetition.

Perhaps involving and teaching parents would be more cost-effective than busing. Dr. Herbert Walberg, an educational psychologist with the University of Chicago, claims that socioeconomic status and family background have much more to do with a child's scholastic achievement than ethnic background. Stability of the home and good parenting are the primary influences that make for quality students, not controlling the percentage of African-American versus white students. That there are better answers than school integration is proven, in special situations, by the largely indistinguishable achievements of African-American and white students who come from like socioeconomic levels. The typical middle class values that derive from strong family ties, a good work ethic, and normal self-esteem make for good academic achievement. Students of Asian background achieve at very satisfactory levels, probably because of a higher level of parental guidance. Certainly, there are better answers.

The United States Department of Education requires schools receiving Title I funds for disadvantaged children to spend 1 percent of that money on parent programs. Title I funding of such programs amounts to but $80 million, which when distributed over the entire country affords but small allotments to local school districts. It is money so well spent that it would justify expanding the program many-fold. Parent programs can be used not only to enhance student learning but also to improve child-parent relationships if done well. Homework assignments are not only on the increase, but homework is often assigned in a format that requires parental involvement. Some schools require parents to sign a form indicating awareness of and involvement with their children's homework and invite constructive comments. In

Bethesda, Maryland, the county government funds homework clubs that provide monitored study; it also makes available a cable-television hotline source for homework help. Homework can be of greater benefit if the schools and teachers are sensitive to the varying abilities of students and parents to cooperate.

Because students in private schools generally achieve at higher levels than students in public schools and have fewer behavioral problems, there is a growing popular opinion favoring private schools. Certainly, these advantages result, at least in part, from high tuition costs for private schools, attracting students from a higher socioeconomic level. This is partially offset by the practice of most private schools to seek diversity through the judicious use of scholarships, but those scholarships are awarded to students who are chosen carefully.

At least four states now allow what are referred to as charter schools, which are given a charter to operate in conformance with preset standards and are paid a sum, sometimes exceeding $5,000, for each student enrolled.

In Michigan, a highly respected African-American woman, Dr. Freya Rivers, began a charter school primarily catering to African-American students and conducted with an African-American heritage theme. The same courses as those in a public school are taught, but the students dress in African-style clothes and learn African history before the history of other cultures. Presumably this approach enhances self-esteem, not only for students but also for parents.

Dr. Rivers limited the school enrollment to 200 at that time, and her students were achieving at much higher levels than are students in the regular public schools. She said that the students in her school, Sankofa Schule, are from average economic and social backgrounds. They even include a typical percentage of children with learning difficulties, who are given the same educational exposure as other students and who soon learn to compete. This probably requires some tender loving motivation on the part of dedicated teachers, but think of the long-term benefits.

Dr. Rivers formerly was a frustrated Lansing public school teacher, but she now enjoys a high level of psychic reward – the result of her ongoing success. Such schooling experiments deserve considerable study by educators and politicians everywhere. They, too, show that school integration, as now implemented, is not the best way. The fact is, although integration was well intended it is broke; further, it was predestined to fail because of poor planning, no statement of mission, and poor communication. Dr. Rivers' success does not mean that we should necessarily abandon integrated schools. We should learn from it, however, and change our integrated schools based on what her experience teaches.

When I interviewed her and suggested that her success was largely due to better parent involvement than exists in public schools, she was quick to point out that when she taught in public schools, she enjoyed over 90 percent parental involvement. Because of her ability and pleasant demeanor, such cooperation is easy to understand. Possibly, however, the parental cooperation her Sankofa Schule enjoys is superior to that which she had in public school because of the pride parents take in her school. Perhaps, too, Dr. Rivers has been able to choose exceptional teachers for her school, a privilege that is difficult to enjoy in the public school domain. With good parental involvement and a small-school atmosphere, it certainly is much easier to control behavioral patterns. We know that when much of a teacher's time is consumed in trying to control classroom behavior, schooling becomes much less effective.

In his annual address to Congress early in February, 1997, President Clinton referred to charter schools and expressed an intention to do what he could to increase their number. Certainly he had all these factors in mind; but, were charter schools to become a dominant influence in our country's educational system, what would the remaining public schools be like? Would a strong swing to charter schools create an unplanned, but sizeable, underprivileged body of public school students? This subject is discussed further in Topic 7, "Integration".

It should be noted that not all charter schools have been successful, and some African-American community leaders oppose them. Perhaps finding people with the unusual talents of Dr. Rivers is extremely difficult.

One of the few programs in the field of education directly funded by government is Head Start started during President Lyndon Johnson's administration. Head Start helps a great deal in preparing a disadvantaged preschool child for school. The National Head Start Association (NHSA. org) reports that Children who participate in Head Start (approximately 700,000 in number) achieve at a higher level on several dimensions than children who are candidates but do not attend Head Start. These dimensions include graduation rates, college attendance rates, lower delinquency and crime rates, fewer teen pregnancies and less dependence on welfare. "Results", a Washington, D.C. organization that lobbies for children's welfare, reports that every dollar invested in early childhood education saves seven dollars in later costs for special education, economic aid, or law enforcement. Head Start is truly cost-effective. In spite of that, short-sighted (or, should we say, non-thinking) members of our House of Representatives are in favor of sharply reducing funding for this program as part of an attempt to balance our national budget.

In an August 1995 issue of *The Wall Street Journal*, staff reporter Rochelle Sharpe reported on how the states have responded to "Goals 2000", a federally-funded program meant to support bottom-up reform of our schools. "Goals 2000" originated, in concept, during the George Bush administration and, with support by President Clinton, was finally approved by Congress. It required states that wished to take advantage of the program apply for the funds available and agree to apply them in a manner that would lead to the achievement of eight national education goals by the year 2000. Those goals had to do with core subjects such as math, science, and geography, all subjects in which American students were deficient when compared to students in other western countries.

Certainly the intent of "Goals 2000" was laudable, but unfortunately Congress failed to be sufficiently participative with the people. As a result, most people are unaware of the program. But the conservative right, which generally opposes government aid programs, quickly and vehemently denounced it. Their fears border on paranoia.

One aspect of public education that has become a major problem, and is continuing to worsen, is the high cost of special education. Special education is usually required for those students who suffer any of a number of learning, emotional, or physical impairments. Special-education students comprise over 10 percent of all students, and the special education necessary to optimize their scholastic achievement costs, per student, well over twice the cost of educating a non-impaired student. This means that about one-third of our education budget is needed for special education. A large portion of the 10 percent comes from single-parent families. In the Fall 2005, Volume 15/No.2 issue of *The Future of Children*, it is stated that "many single-parents find it difficult to function effectively as parents". It goes on to say that quality parenting is one of the best predictors of a child's well-being. Further evidence of this is the significant reduction in the number of students suffering from learning disabilities when the quality of parenting is improved. In the Springfield, Missouri school system, a practical parenting partnership was implemented which sent teachers into students' homes and brought parents into the schools for parenting skill sessions. As a result, the parenting quality was so improved that the number of sixth graders (for example) who were classified as learning disabled fell from nearly 40 percent to approximately 7.5 percent.

In the Union School District, a suburb of Tulsa, Oklahoma, a program called *Character Counts* has been instituted. It is a program which has been used by many other schools around the country and has also been applied by businesses and law enforcement agencies. *Character Counts* stresses six pillars of virtue: citizenship, respect, responsibility, fairness, caring, and trustworthiness. This program is interwoven throughout the curriculum with reliance on the individual teachers for specific implementation. With civility at an all-time low in our society, it is hoped that this program will be of significant benefit.

The National Institute for Dispute Resolution helps both elementary and secondary schools organize and implement peer mediation programs, which are wonderful programs for resolving student conflicts. In this process, students have demonstrated an ability to vastly improve overall school culture and learn to be much more understanding of each other. The program has been shown to reduce violence, school suspension, and many types of behavioral problems. Peer mediation programs should be implemented at all schools. They work to enhance character because the students participate in solving problems, largely by themselves, but with counseling as needed.

There are many examples of parents, most often mothers, who volunteer as teachers' assistants. They usually enhance the teacher's effectiveness by aiding students who absorb knowledge slowly, thereby accelerating the learning process.

Thomas Friedman, in his book *The World Is Flat*, very convincingly concludes that our educational system is badly flawed and is permitting may other countries to not only approach our standards but in some ways to surpass us. The statistics he has assembled indicate that the number of students receiving advanced education in science and technology in China, India, Russia, for example, far exceeds us, and is quick to point out, in time that will permit those countries to pass us economically. His book is important for our educators and those who control educational funds to study. Further reference to education may be found under Topic 25, "Our Withering Democracy".

Social Security

Demographic trends are causing a gradual increase in the number of seniors on Social Security and, percentagewise, fewer employed people who are paying into Social Security. Although this impending serious problem has been known for some time, Congress has been very slow to give it adequate consideration. In 2008, they finally did act on it by extending the age at which Social Security becomes effective from 65 to 67. This will impact people born after January 1, 1960 and will, no doubt, cause much irritation, when those born the day before the deadline are entitled to Social Security payments at age 65 while those born one day later (perhaps even an hour later) are not entitled to it until age 67. That change will delay the year in which the Social Security system becomes financially unsound, but there has been no indication for it being a long-range answer.

An article, by Allan Sloan, entitled "The Hour Draws Near" in the March 31, 2008 issue of Forbes Magazine, refers to the fact that Social Security has no means for making up the shortfall it will experience by 2020. By "shortfall" he means that at that time the monies being paid into the Social Security fund will be less than it is required to pay out. For the millions of dollars it collected through the years in excess of what it has paid out it has only United States securities, mere paper, unless there is a means of converting them to cash. The government has no way of redeeming those "IOUs" other than borrowing the huge amounts of money required to do so or reducing other spending accordingly. Unless conditions change considerably, inadequate funding could cause Social Security to become a major source of chaos, although the recent revision to retirement age will delay it.

That Social Security has become an indispensable part of our economic well-being is universally accepted. For this reason, it could be calamitous to further delay facing the issue. Doing so will probably result in the usual political confusion and lack of public participation. Were a trained brainstorming leader to lead an unbiased "think tank" group through several sessions of problem solving concerning Social Security, the likely recommendations, or possible solutions, would give both government and the public options to consider. Necessary compromises should be evaluated in a manner that would result in understanding by all and permit a long-range plan implementing such changes with minimum hardship. This process, if properly executed, should also be devoid of political consideration or pandering to the voters. Congress would not have to fear a serious public backlash if understanding has been created for the need of such changes. Further, change could be gradually implemented so as to lessen the severity of impact.

There are at least four types of change that seem possible. One would involve further revision of the age at which Social Security would begin to be paid. The second would increase the maximum yearly wages subject to deduction for Social Security. Of course, that would impact only the higher wage earners. A third possible change would be to increase the percentage paid into Social Security from each paycheck, which might have too great an impact on those at lower wage levels. A fourth type of change would provide that our government pay a more competitive rate of interest for the funds it borrows from Social Security; this would make a marked improvement.

Affirmative Action

Affirmative action does not provide money for direct distribution to those it intends to benefit. For this reason, it is not the typical entitlement. However, it is an organized attempt to: one, improve opportunities available to ethnic minorities, primarily African-Americans, in the areas of business, education, or housing; two, provide equal opportunity for women in the workplace; and three, to hasten the integration of minorities into all phases of our social fabric.

In most respects, unfortunately, this well-meaning legislation has failed to accomplish the intended goals. Few of us would hesitate to relate socially with, "break bread" with, go to school with, or be neighbors with people of other backgrounds regardless of a difference in skin color or nationality. We do, however, attach much importance to cultural compatibility. Yes, the efforts of affirmative action have resulted in more rapid change for the better than might have occurred otherwise, but the basic problems remain unsolved. An unintended backlash is now developing because, at times minorities are given preference over more qualified whites so that affirmative action targets can be met. This backlash has also been expressed by students who have not been able to attain acceptance by their college of choice while minorities with lesser qualifications have been accepted. The courts are now evaluating such claims. In his book "My American Journey", Colin Powell emphatically states, "Equal rights and equal opportunity mean just that. They do not mean preferential treatment. Preferences, no matter how well intended, ultimately breed resentment among the non-preferred. Affirmative Action, in the best sense, should promote equal consideration, not reverse discrimination".

California has enacted Proposition 209, which makes race and gender preferences and quotas illegal in public education. This Civil Rights initiative has been upheld by an appeals court and is a model for many such initiatives around the country. The long-term effect of Proposition 209 is not yet clear, but already some state universities are observing that there are fewer minorities in their recent freshman classes. Those white applicants who were previously left out in favor of minority applicants who qualified for admittance only because of affirmative action edicts, not because they were more qualified, certainly had reason to feel they were unjustly treated. Proposition 209 will rectify their complaints. Obviously, if we wish to have African-Americans and other minorities achieve college degrees in greater numbers, the problem requires other solutions. At some universities Asian students are overrepresented. If they have gained admission solely based on their scholastic merit, fine, but their being favored for any other reason is not defensible.

As noted by columnist Thomas Sowell in an article dated June 4th, 2002 in *Capital Magazine,* he referred to the large increase in the number of minority students attending the University of California at Irvine since the enactment of Proposition 209. Prior to that event, universities with academic programs that were more challenging than that of the University of California at Irvine were required to admit many minority students who were really unqualified to withstand the more severe academic programs at UCLA, for example. Most minority students who might have been unable to make it at UCLA are doing well at Irvine and graduate prepared to do better in the job market than they might have done after being unsuccessful in a tougher academic environment.

In 1981, the city of Birmingham, Alabama was required to gradually make its municipal work force reflect the area's population makeup - then 43 percent female and 27 percent African-American. White firefighters sued and, after a 1989 Supreme Court ruling in their favor, challenged the city's affirmative action plan. As a result, in December 1995, a federal judge ordered the city to develop a new non-discriminatory hiring process within four years that would utilize selection procedures that either have no negative impact based on sex or race or are job-related and consistent with business necessity. Probably this latest court action will require further definition as implementation proceeds, but hiring minorities based on percentages has not worked as intended.

In 1995, the Dynalantic Corp. was prevented from bidding on flight simulators for the Huey helicopter. The government had reserved the contract for minority-owned companies. Dynalantic Corp. challenged that decision and a circuit court held in its favor. The majority of judges on the court decreed that it was unconstitutional to show such preferential treatment even though it might be considered merely benign discrimination. There also are many instances of misapplied affirmative action in which government contracts have been awarded to organizations especially formed for the purpose of taking advantage of former preferential treatment of minority-owned companies. In such organizations, there ostensibly was minority leadership, but, in fact, there would be non-minority silent partners who had financial control and expected to receive most of the financial rewards. Again, the intended preferential consideration toward minorities in awarding government contracts was good, but the implementation process was flawed and permitted much abuse. Perhaps if there was a requisite minimum of three years of business success (for example), it could be considered within the spirit of the Constitution if a minority organization were awarded a contract over a non-minority bidder but only if such bidders were equally qualified and equally able to guarantee quality and performance.

An installment of the comic strip "Blondie" depicts Blondie endeavoring to secure a permit to remodel her shop. After expressing her frustration over the red tape to an officious clerk at the license bureau, she angrily states, "And I am an American citizen! What if I were a foreigner?" The clerk replies, "Then we could help you". Although this is only comic strip humor, Blondie's frustration is typical of that felt by many a citizen who feels that affirmative action has become very annoying.

Even the ability to communicate verbally becomes a consideration in our attitudes toward minorities. Many of us have difficulty empathizing with people who are born and raised in America but who have difficulty communicating in English. A friend of mine who is an executive with an international firm based in London has told me that his company does not hire people who speak with a cockney accent because their foreign employees, customers, and suppliers all have difficulty communicating with someone who has a cockney accent. In that case minorities are not involved, but it points out that communicative abilities, which are a factor in our attitudes toward affirmative action in the United States are also a source of difficulty elsewhere. It is reasonable to assume that international companies based in the United States might also be uncomfortable having employees with bad Brooklyn or deep Southern accents. Fortunately, there are good schools available to those who want to replace their cockney accent in England with the Queen's English and good schools of diction in the United States.

A report in *Chicago Policy Review, 1998* by Steve Russell entitled American Indians in the Twilight of Affirmative Action states "the group at statistical bottom of all the scales thought to measure lack of opportunity is American Indians". That report indicates that the number of businesses owned by American Indians and Alaska Natives increased 115 percent from 1987 to 1992 and the total receipts for those businesses increased 115 percent during that period. These indicators of economic progress by American Indians have been aided by many affirmative action programs that included "recruitment, outreach, training, and educational initiatives". But, the American Indian is still far behind almost all other ethnic groups.

One relatively recent movement to aid them economically is American Indian owned casinos. In 1988 Congress passed the Indian Gaming Regulation Act which allowed American Indians to establish and run gambling casinos. It was not Congress' intent to primarily aid the large numbers of American Indians who have already done well financially but who are only marginally Indian, a result of a few hundred years of integration, but that has happened nonetheless.

There are now so many such casinos spread over the United States, according to internet access of The *Time Archive* (an internet accessible encyclopedic compilation of almost fifty years of information derived from *Time Magazine*) their total revenues exceed the sum of all Las Vegas casinos plus Atlantic City casino revenues. By law Indian Casinos must be built on land that is owned by them and not more than 40 percent of the net revenues can go to outside investors. Even though these rules are flagrantly violated, as indicated in *The Time Archive*, enough benefit does flow to the tribes to improve their living standards considerably although not near enough to erase the large disparity between their lack of financial well-being and that of the American population-at-large. Indian tribes often do not have to subscribe to the tax laws that apply to other Americans which is often irritating when they are then accused of unfair competition by businesses that are not Indian owned. An example of this problem is in the sale of cigarettes to which they do not apply the same excise tax burden.

Referring to Indian Casinos, The Time Archive also headlines one report "Look who's cashing in. Hint: it's not the people who are supposed to benefit". Overall the Indian Gaming Regulation Act as established by Congress is another example of how easy it is for politicians to turn concept into chaos.

Although standards of performance sometimes have had to be lowered as a result of affirmative action, were there positive long-term trends resulting from affirmative action, such negative effects could be rationalized as being temporary. Such is not the case, and those who have been able to overcome and successfully adapt, economically and culturally, probably would have done so on their own, albeit less easily, without the tremendous expense of affirmative action programs.

Affirmative action treats symptoms but leaves the causes of such problems unaddressed. Only a few programs, such as Head Start and school lunch programs are directed at causes, and these are not implemented in such a manner as to be as effective as they might be. In the attempt to optimize national budgetary considerations, even these programs are likely to be cut back.

Another type of affirmative action sets guidelines or targets for industry with regard to helping minorities become managers or owners of businesses. As part of its effort to satisfy both the public and government with regard to minority ownership of its automobile dealerships, the Ford Motor Company recruited Samuel Foster, an African-American North Carolina businessman, to purchase a Ford dealership in Selma, Alabama. Three years later, that dealership failed financially, and Foster sued Ford with the claim that it had committed intentional, malicious fraud by failing to inform him that African-Americans had a higher than average likelihood of failure. The jury agreed and Mr. Foster was subsequently awarded six million dollars in punitive damages, seven hundred thousand for mental anguish, and almost one million for economic loss. An important aspect of that case is that Mr. Foster's partner in this venture, Mr. Deewitt Sperau, who is white, apparently will share in the awards. The Alabama Supreme Court has concurred that Ford is culpable. It certainly seems beyond the original intent of the law that Ford was not only obligated to recruit minority owners of their dealerships but also, in a very paternalistic way, to aid them in managing those dealerships to assure profitability. The fact that Mr. Foster had a white partner seems to have been overlooked.

Certainly, corporations wishing to comply with the intent of affirmative action by establishing minority-owned dealerships have problems they had not previously imagined as a result of the Alabama court decision against Ford. The overwhelming possibility exists, in the foregoing instance, that what seems to be grossly unfair jurisprudence is another instance of the failure of our imperiled jury system to cope with the ability of some attorneys to successfully play on juries' emotions in a manner that warps their thinking.

In 1985, several prominent African-American individuals were given a considerable tax break in their purchase of a Buffalo, New York television station which they since have sold for a handsome profit. Although the government's supposed intent was to aid disadvantaged African-American people, such was not the case when the investors included O.J. Simpson, Colin Powell, Patrick Ewing, Julius

Erving, actor Mr. T, and members of Michael Jackson's family. None of those would be considered disadvantaged. In fact, most were probably millionaires at the time.

In 1988, Congress passed the Indian Gaming Regulation Act, which allowed American Indians to establish and run gambling casinos, providing they could first obtain permission from their states. It was not Congress' intent to aid the embarrassingly large percentage of impoverished who have gotten rich but are only marginally Indian, a result of a few hundred years of integration. Those who have become affluent often branch out into other businesses that compete regionally in an unfair manner in that they are not required to file public financial statements and are not subject to the same tax laws. This overall situation is another example of how easy it is for our government to turn concept into chaos.

Many ethnic groups have successfully overcome language, educational, and financial barriers. That they have done so is indicated by their academic, social, and economic achievements. Perhaps Congress would benefit from studying why some ethnic groups have been so successful while others have failed and modify their programs to incorporate this learning as a result.

Certainly in its attempt to benefit society with affirmative action programs, our government is failing miserably. Yes, there is need for social welfare of the kind intended by affirmative action, but the approach needs better planning than our untrained politicians seem capable of, regardless of their good intentions. That the manner in which they use research committees and consulting groups is very flawed is proven by the results. The overall government affirmative action effort needs to be reviewed and severely modified, but it would seem very wrong to eliminate it rather than fix it.

Conclusions

All of the foregoing programs are in need of review and change. At the time of this writing, Congress is in the throes of such a review with the goal of reducing the overall cost of welfare programs to the federal government by reducing program benefits or passing responsibility to the individual states. Such thinking, unfortunately, accompanies their urgent need to reduce the federal budget. As in the past, they are not studying the problems with a historical perspective. They have permitted abuses to continue too long, and their actions seem to highlight some aspects of the problems and completely neglect others. An example of this is their consideration of what to do with the many programs relating to the working poor, the unemployed poor, those receiving food stamps, aid to families with dependent children, and school lunch programs. They seem bent on "passing the buck" by shoving responsibility down to the states. No doubt they will then brag about having reduced the cost of federal government even though the tax payers may have to pay as much or more, to provide such programs at the state level.

Such changes, without sufficient planning, may result in severe disruption to those receiving benefits. Were the states required to administer programs transferred to them in accordance with established federal guidelines, perhaps good quality control could be maintained. Without such control, history has shown that the states will conduct them with a wide variance in quality and often with an even larger percentage of the cost being absorbed by administrative expense.

The need to balance our federal budget, without having to include as income our payments into Social Security, is certainly urgent. The magnitude of the problem is probably much greater than we are led to believe, since the imbalance we are told of is merely the negative yearly federal cash flow. If the government had to include in its financial reporting all those items which are referred to as "off budget", such as unfunded retirement funds, our federal financial statement might show us to be irretrievably bankrupt. Such criticism may seem unduly severe when the national indebtedness of so many other countries represents a higher percentage of their overall economy than is true of the United States. However, there should be little solace in having so much company who also are in sad financial condition.

6. Welfare and Poverty

Too often, it is assumed that the typical welfare recipient is lazy and unemployable. Certainly there are those "on the dole" who are considered pathologically dependent, although even many of those people can be given employment at less than challenging jobs. Yes, doing so may require pay scale compromises and the continuing need for some supplemental welfare, but there would be the psychological benefit of enhanced self-esteem and a reduction in welfare bureaucracy.

In 1996, Congress passed a law providing that employers who had hired workers previously on welfare would be eligible for tax credits of up to $8,500. That spawned the subsequent formation of an organization called the "Welfare to Work Partnership". That organization has a volunteer full-time director and a board of directors made up of officers from major corporations who take their responsibilities seriously.

During the Great Depression of the 1930s, the Roosevelt administration established the WPA (Works Project Administration). It initiated construction projects to build roads, parks, public buildings, and many other types of useful public entities. In doing so, large numbers of jobs were created, people learned new trades, welfare was reduced, and our country has benefited ever since from the good work that resulted. Perhaps a study should be made to see if a WPA-type organization would be practical today.

Certainly, working for a living wage, even if arranged for by government, is vastly superior to being "on the dole" and much more constructive in terms of one's self-esteem. There surely is so much need to improve our infrastructure that a list of such projects would be almost endless. At least we would be getting something for our money.

In my work with the Mental Health Organization in Tulsa, Oklahoma, I have learned that many people on welfare are classified as mentally ill. Not enough effort is made to make appropriate help available to them. It has been shown that with proper treatment, both psychological and medical, most of them can be placed in supervised group housing and taught self-sufficiency in a manner that soon permits them to rejoin society and, with a continuing maintenance program, become self-sufficient. One of the most successful programs of this type is under the auspices of our Mental Health Organization in Tulsa. Its goal is to completely eliminate homelessness in Tulsa, which is primarily made up of people sleeping "on the streets".

Since over 20 percent of our population suffers, in varying degrees, from mental illness or depression, such homelessness has become a major problem. In May 2008 television news investigators reported a new type of homeless people – those who are living in their cars because of financial inability to provide housing for themselves. Such people may indeed need counseling and welfare assistance, but they would not be classified as mentally ill.

In August of 2008 the United States Census Bureau released its 2007 data on poverty, income, and health insurance. It indicated that the number of poor people rose by 816,000. The poverty rate in 2007 was 12.5 percent versus

11.7 percent in 2001. During that interval, median income for working households declined $1,100. Also during that interval, the number of people without health insurance increased from 39.8 million to 45.7 million. Such negative trends, if not properly addressed, can certainly lead to an increased need for welfare, as well as other chaotic conditions.

7. Integration

Integration is the process by which those who have different cultural backgrounds blend into a society. When people have difficulty doing so, society should aid and encourage this blending process. Most government actions in that regard do have this intention, even though most fall short of this desired goal. Integrated housing, which finally is occurring in many parts of the country, seems to have the effect of reducing cultural identity for African-Americans. For that reason, there are many who criticize it. They say that although immigrants from other countries are able to retain their cultural identity and sense of history, African-Americans tend to lose theirs with integrated housing. As a result, those who achieve success leaving the fold, often consider themselves separated from and above those who have not done so, although close family relationships usually prevent this social problem. In her book *Miz Lucy's Cookies,* Eddie Faye Gates refers to successful African-Americans leaving the fold and the serious decay in the quality of family relationships among African-Americans. Unfortunately, this is not a problem that only government should address. It should also be addressed by the African-American community itself, especially by those African-Americans who have achieved success.

We can observe integration efforts in several fields, including the military, sports, housing, industry, and schools. Some of them are working; some are not. Those that are working are doing so with teenagers and adults who are integrated with a team approach in which there is participative involvement, at least to the point of encouraging individual decisions such as "this will be beneficial for me". Those efforts that are not working do not properly encourage participation by all involved which, unfortunately, is too often the case in public schools. As shown by the failure in California of their former policy of admitting college applicants based on ethnic percentages, integration based on numerical goals usually backfires. If the integration process is not governed well, it becomes little more than an exercise in diversity accompanied by many negative results.

In the military, each soldier is soon convinced that, in battle, one's life depends on those soldiers who surround him or her. That realization and shared understanding of the common goals create a "sense of family". Identification by skin color or ethnic background is deeply sublimated. As a result, integration in the military is highly successful at all levels, even having produced General Colin Powell, an African-American, as Chairman of our Joint Chiefs of Staff, with responsibility for all branches of our military until his retirement from that position in 1993. Integration of our huge Hispanic population, which is largely made up of Mexicans, is a different problem entirely. That segment of our society is estimated at over twelve million and is a subject of much argument because so many are in the United States unlawfully. Further, our border with Mexico remains permeable to illegal immigration. That this is also true of our Canadian border which can make us more vulnerable to terrorism. Illegal entry by Canadians has been no problem thus far. The economy of Canada is very much like ours. They do not have a large percentage of their population unemployed or below a poverty line as is the case in Mexico.

Congress has recently taken the step of requiring passports of all United States citizens when leaving our country. Previously that was not a requirement when traveling to Canada or several Caribbean islands. Because enactment of that change overloaded passport issuing offices, many applicants found their travel plans in jeopardy because their passport requests were not expected to be filled until after their scheduled departure date. That situation caused the effective date for this change to be postponed for several months. It was not the most serious mistake in the world, but it is another example of inadequate planning.

The big debates on how to tighten our border with Mexico to prevent unlawful entry and what to do about the millions who are already here unlawfully have not produced answers. The situation is so complex as to almost defy solution. It certainly will require a lot of compromise, especially by the hard-liners who are totally intolerant of the idea of amnesty being granted to those already, here even though there is general consensus that we cannot ship twelve million people back to Mexico. Congress, for a change, needs to act on this problem with long-term fairness and in the best interests of the United States without pandering to any segment of the public–and the sooner the better. Everyone in congress knows we cannot deport twelve million illegal Mexicans, but pressured by the large number of citizens opposed to any form or degree of amnesty, they have abdicated their duty and shelved any action indefinitely.

Virtually all Mexicans who come to the United States, legally or illegally, do so to escape the poverty they suffered in Mexico. On almost any day there will be a line two blocks long around the United States Consulate in Mexico City of people attempting to obtain legal entry into the United States. Very few are successful in this mission. Therefore, unable to escape their entrapment in permanent poverty, many people use illegal means to seek refuge in the United States. Many lives are lost in this process, but large numbers do succeed. They find menial jobs here which United States citizens try to avoid because of the low wages available. These wages, however, are considerably higher than those at home, and they enable laborers to send money to their families in Mexico. This transfer of monies to Mexican families at home is estimated to exceed $20 billion per year – a very substantial sum that is not usually mentioned in the halls of Congress. That people do send money home, even though they have little to spare, shows they have love of family. In addition, the close bond they often form with American families is further evidence that they are, for the most part, good people even though they are here illegally. Unfortunately, they often suffer from bad treatment, especially from our police, who, based on mere suspicion that they are here illegally, frequently arrest them for traffic violations and turn them over to Immigration authorities. Such police action, although justified, too often results in their being deported without having been made aware of legal defense actions available to them. This can and does occur without notification of family, perhaps leaving a spouse and children without means of support.

Were we to truly stop illegal immigration at the border, the problems outlined might disappear within a generation or so, but without border control the problem will continue to worsen ad infinitum. Presumably, we are trying to improve border control by building a high fence along our Mexican border, a project that as of this writing is proceeding at a rate of about one mile per month. At that rate it may never become effective. The military has found that a second, parallel fence offers exponential benefit in that, whereas a single fence will still permit escapees, a double fence reduces the number to virtually zero. We are not using this military approach.

Thus far, Mexico is doing nothing to help us control the problem, and no wonder when they benefit from it all. They have fewer poverty stricken citizens to worry about and their economy is benefiting from the twenty billion dollars they gain each year.

8. Crime

In the United States, by the mid-1990s, crime had reached a level that would have seemed unbelievable to our grandparents, who often lived with unlocked doors and could walk the streets at night without qualm. Today, anger, violence, and random and unlawful use of knives and guns are but part of an atmosphere so full of crime as to give many of us a feeling of paranoia. Statistics, which often can be compiled to reflect a variety of results, indicate that some types of crime are now declining, but subsequent studies show that accompanying such declines is a much larger prison population and the treatment of teenagers as adults in some states. The United States Justice Department's Bureau of Justice Statistics reports that the United States rate of incarceration nearly doubled in the ten-year period ending in December, 1995. There is little evidence that keeping people in prison has any great beneficial influence on their ethics or behavior patterns.

Quoting the New York Times News Service, an article in the Tulsa World (an Oklahoma newspaper) dated April 22nd, 1996 states that a comprehensive report on the overall cost of crime in the United States, ordered by the Justice Department, indicates that crime costs us approximately $450 billion per year. This study includes both direct and indirect costs. Although direct costs are relatively well understood, we usually fail to realize that crime also engenders many indirect costs for those who are its victims.

Indirect costs would include the cost of crime prevention, extra security measures, lost work time, legal fees, and various intangibles such as counseling often required by the victims of crime. Most of this indirect cost is not borne by government and, therefore, does not affect our tax burden. The out-of-pocket expenses suffered by the average rape victim exceed $5,000, and that does not include the long-term effect of mental anguish on the victim's quality of life.

Many retailers find it necessary to increase the price of goods sold by as much as five percent to cover inventory losses and theft prevention costs. The huge overall cost of crime, if reduced merely 50 percent (including indirect costs), would produce savings of half of $450 billion of direct costs and my estimate of an equal amount of indirect costs. Certainly such savings would alleviate our national budget problems appreciably. These figures need to be given greater publicity, to give the public better perspective when next considering the tax impact of any proposed anti-crime legislation. The expenditures represented by the most recent anti-crime bills enacted by Congress were, literally, insignificant compared to the cost of crime.

Certainly, justice, even to those who are criminals, is important, but to those of us who fear walking the streets at night, there seems to be a marked imbalance in favor of the criminal in recent legislation. William Bennett, in his book *The Index of Leading Cultural Indicators,* noted that in 1990, punishment for murder averaged 1.8 years of imprisonment, sixty days for rape, twenty-three days for robbery, and but 6.4 days for aggravated assault. He states that fewer than one in ten serious crimes in the United States results in prison time. Of course, these statistics perhaps are warped by those crimes he included which did not result in prosecution by the victim or in conviction. It would seem, however, that his research was adequate to prove that our system of justice is a farce, which seemed evident during the television spectacle of the O. J. Simpson trial.

Virtually nothing is being done to reduce the number of criminals, long-term; and, short-term, criminals who are apprehended and brought to justice too often are out on the streets in a very short time without any change in behavioral pattern. Try to convince a criminal who again resorts to his previous criminal habits after but a short stay in prison that crime does not pay!

The current trend to carry arms in self-defense may very well benefit the munitions manufacturers who finance the National Rifle Association's vast influence, but in the opinion of most sociologists and criminologists, we are creating a potential monster that does not reduce crime at all. It has been called, by some, a "redneck" response to crime. This trend to carry arms now includes machine-gun-like automatic weapons capable of firing dozens of bullets per minute.

Tom McNichol, a writer for *USA Weekend,* tells the story of Ms. Joyce Strickland, whose son was shot and killed in a Dallas robbery. As head of Mothers Against Teen Violence, she opposes new laws that permit issuing licenses to carry concealed weapons. She says, "If gun violence were a medical disease our children were dying of, there would be a nationwide effort to find a cure".

To date, much attention has been given to incarcerating criminals, and the capacity of our prison system is increasing rapidly. The growth rate of crime exceeds the growth of our prisons, however, and without minimizing the importance of imprisoning violent criminals, it seems fair to say that this will not solve our crime problem. Further, it should be noted that an appreciable percentage of people serving time are guilty of victimless crimes. Reducing the causes of criminal behavior seems to be a more likely approach for reducing crime, but politics keep getting in the way.

Reported by Natalie Angier in the New York Times Service, in 1995, Dr. David Wasserman a legal scholar at the University of Maryland organized a conference to discuss "the meaning and significance of research on genetics and criminal behavior". The organizers couched the description of their conference-to-be in words that would be least apt to offend the many obstructionists they envisioned. Sure enough, there was such outrage caused by the possibility of their concluding that crime could be a genetically inbred trait that the National Institute of Health had to renege on its agreement to provide a grant that would partially finance the conference. African-American organizations were also vociferous in their condemnation of such a conference. Somehow, because of Dr. Wasserman's persistence and that of the University, the conference was held thanks to the reinstated support of the National Institute of Health. The results of the meeting have not been published as of this writing, but the fact is that recognized behavioral experts do consider genetics to be a possible factor in crime. Since these results and the methods used in reaching their conclusions are unpublished, we do not know whether or not social environment was isolated as a factor. Given a sufficiently large sampling of people of various racial backgrounds, all from like educational levels and comparable living standards, would genetics then be as likely to be a factor. I have read a considerable number of studies having to do with the possible link of genetics and the propensity to crime and have yet to find any definitive conclusions. There are and probably will continue to be more studies in this field, but thus far all the evidence is inconclusive.

Certainly, a much greater influence on the propensity toward crime is social environment, which can include parenting, education, deprivation, and drugs. Much could be done to improve the quality of parenting and education, and to reduce deprivation. In turn, dependence on drugs would be reduced markedly. Yes, children from fine homes partake of drugs, and being from a "good home" does not necessarily equate to having had good parenting; and, yes, sometimes even good parenting does not prevent drug use due to peer pressure. However, good parenting would surely reduce the effect of peer pressure. Politics and organized religious groups are often impediments to any corrective efforts in the areas of parenting and education. Progress, in these areas, only seems to emanate from volunteer-type nonprofit organizations, and such efforts are insufficient.

To mention the importance of parenting without reference to the prevalence of child abuse would be a severe oversight. This is especially highlighted by the following statistics indicating percentages of sociopaths (people characterized by antisocial behavior) that were abused as children:

- 78 percent of prison inmates
- 80 percent of substance abusers
- 80 percent of prostitutes
- 95 percent of sex offenders
- 97 percent of juvenile delinquents

These statistics vary from one area of the country to another and are certainly influenced by the quality of education. No wonder our efforts at reducing crime are so ineffective. We are doing so little to improve the quality of parenting. Government sponsored social welfare programs do try to fight deprivation, but such programs are doomed to continual failure without fighting the battle on the parenting and educational fronts at the same time.

An article in *The Wall Street Journal* of July 27, 1995 depicted in considerable detail how United States Marine recruits at Parris Island, South Carolina become physically fit, drug-free, well-behaved, self-disciplined, courteous, and virtually free of racial prejudice in a period of but eleven weeks. Not only are those who receive such training less apt to be sociopathic, but they are also likely to enjoy happier lives. At the outset of such training, the typical group includes social misfits, drug users, gang activists, and those with a completely negative attitude toward the future. We can remember a period during the Second World War during which most of our able-bodied men were drafted into the military. That experience did, in fact, have a positive influence in all these areas of behavior. Even today, there are examples of the psychological benefits to the individual from military training, Israel being a good example. In Israel virtually everyone is required to serve in the military. Certainly, the cost of such military-like training might seem justified, especially long-term, because of the resulting reduced cost of government entitlements and penal systems. This would enhance our military preparedness as well. That avenue of thinking may or may not be a way to go, but it is deserving of non-political discussion with the primary consideration being, "Would it be of long-term benefit to our country?"

Early in 1992, a state attorney in Jacksonville, Florida, where violent crime had reached a very high level, began a program that treated juvenile criminals as adults subject to incarceration, whereas they previously had been placed on probation in consideration of their age. That change resulted in a large percentage of juvenile criminals being taken off the streets and a 30 percent decrease in juvenile arrests. Similar results have been reported in many cities, including some that have reputations for high violent crime rates. Professor John Dilulio, Jr. of Princeton University advised in the early 1990s that by the year 2000 there will be an increase of 500,000 teenaged males in our population, a group that would likely provide us with 30,000 more young murderers, muggers, and rapists. That statistic assumed that the percentages heretofore prevalent would not get worse, which he thought unlikely. He opined that such statistics are nearly ordained by the swelling numbers of children who are growing up fatherless, Godless, jobless, and undisciplined.

Between 1992 and 1995, Texas tripled its prison system, adding nearly 100,000 more beds. The cost of this expansion exceeded $1.5 billion. It resulted in prisoners serving a much greater percentage of their sentence, resulting in paroles being granted at only one-fourth of the previous frequency. No longer were so many paroles necessary in order to make room for new prisoners. Texas was criticized in many circles for this "hard-nosed" approach to crime, but the resulting reduction in crime has motivated the state government into a further expansion of its prison system. From the time these new prison facilities have become available, the reduction of crime in Texas has been approximately double the reduction nationwide. Perhaps longer periods of incarceration would permit a better approach to rehabilitation and a major reduction in recidivism. In Section IX, Topic 36, "Non-linear Planning," crime is discussed in further detail.

While on the subject of crime, it is important to assume that a person who has been pardoned or has completed a prison sentence is deserving of a new chance in life. In addition, there are a few who are later proven innocent and others who are basically good people but were unduly influenced by peer pressure. In my former company we had two people, who had been guilty of a previous crime, and became highly valued and trusted employees.

9. Domestic Mores and Value Systems

In the past fifteen years there has been an increase of over 25 percent in the number of children who are being raised by grandparents. When the reason for grandparents being put in the position of having to care for their grandchildren has to do with immorality or neglectfulness on the part of the parents, the children are often better off being raised by their grandparents. In fact, under such circumstances the respect and love from their grandparents is usually quite high. Often parents who cannot properly perform their parenting responsibilities are involved with drugs, are incarcerated, have had a child out of wedlock, or have some other inexcusable reason.

The percentage of children being raised in single-parent homes is now huge and growing. The United States Census Bureau indicated in 1997 that among mothers with children under six years old, 85 percent of African-Americans, 73 percent of Hispanics, and 56 percent of whites have never been married. To people who were born before 1950, such percentages seem almost unbelievable and reflect a rather sick society. Such children frequently are relegated to child care centers, many of which are profit-oriented with little attention given to nurturing social skills and good education. Older children, who attend public schools, often return to an empty home after school and are left to their own devices until the parent returns home from work. The parent, after a day's work, is usually tired and then has to prepare dinner and perform myriad household duties. Spending quality time with the child or children is virtually impossible. Lacking the balanced exposure of being raised by both a mother and a father, such children have less than a good start in life.

Homes in which both parents work often suffer from the same problems, in that the children may be unsupervised during most of the day. Yes, when working parents can provide a trained nanny to supervise and feed their children during their absence, a vastly improved set of circumstances can exist, but economics make such conditions prohibitive for most families in which both parents work. A few generations ago, when it was uncommon to find families with both parents working, the quality of parenting was relatively superior, and we had much less teenage crime and higher scholastic achievement.

Although there are exceptions, when most of us leave this earth, our most important bequest to the world will be our children. How much money we made or what our vocation may have been, in most cases, will soon be forgotten. But having left behind good children who have respected ethical values and who contribute to society in a positive manner, the world will be better off for our having been part of it. The percentage of families regarded by sociologists as dysfunctional is much too high and indirectly contributes to many of our social ills. The 2000 Census figures indicate that over 60% of families suffer or have suffered parental separation and 72% harbor someone with an addiction. There is no substitute for good parenting. If all peoples of the world were raised with good parenting, many of our world's ills would be largely non-existent.

Early in the twentieth century it was common for high schools to have a required course in Civics. Students in the class would have to choose one or two well-regarded area newspapers, study the editorials and participate in class discussion. Impartially guided by the teacher, the class would be led into discussions having to do with ethics and civility. The teacher did not knowingly foster attitudes, but the ensuing discussions stimulated minds and evoked penetrating thought. Educators thought that much beneficial teenage maturing resulted from such a class. Today, such a school activity would be nearly impossible because of parental fears that their children might learn something unacceptable. – especially among people of evangelical faiths. This author participated in such a class and is unaware of any student or parent who can look back and say that it was anything but constructive. That was an era in which civility and good behavior were at very high level compared to the present. It was an era in which children were trusted with knowledge that then, or later, permitted them to make wiser decisions–a basis for creativity.

10. International Relationships and Value Systems

Value systems and rules of courtesy vary from country to country, and it is important for those involved in international trade or diplomacy to be aware of the differences before traveling internationally. This is becoming more important as technology makes the world seem smaller. When individuals, businesses, and governments conduct themselves in a manner that enhances mutual respect and friendship among nations, the likelihood of chaos that results from international confrontation is reduced. To this end, not only is good conduct important, but understanding the heritage, viewpoints, and needs of people from other cultures is equally important.

This topic is of importance in that international understanding and relationships can exert a strong influence on the peace process. They also influence the manner in which nations learn from each other, which is of profound long-term importance. As we become internationally "homogenized", interdependence will deepen and mores will gradually change and be less apt to contribute to misunderstandings. Because international conflict can be one of the worst sources of chaos, perhaps, in the future, our high schools can find a way to include an abbreviated study of international cultures and economies.

The tendency for the world to become "homogenized" is evident, and even languages are gradually intertwining. This is occurring slowly, but it will, nonetheless, have a positive long-term effect. Increases in travel and the large numbers of students studying in countries other than their own contribute to this. To the degree that this is so, it justifies our encouraging foreign students to study in the United States, provided that we keep insurrectionists from doing so.

In his book *The World Is Flat,* Thomas Friedman logically presents his analysis of the vast impact computers are having on our world. The percentage of people who are "computer savvy" over much of the world is almost unbelievable. This degree of sophistication has an important "homogenizing" influence and may even result in improved international relations as the younger computer users graduate to become leaders in their respective countries. Their ongoing communication activities over the Internet should make for better understanding and less divisiveness. Fortunately, such Internet communication is difficult to control or eliminate as dictator-type governments attempt to do.

11. Civility and Cordiality

In other portions of this book I mention a decline in the quality of interpersonal relationships. A former Nebraska football coach, Tom Osborn, asserts "There has been a marked decline in the behavioral pattern of his available recruits". His observation is true not only of available football recruits but also of people at large in our country and in many other parts of the world. This trend is accompanied by a large decline in civility and a rise in bad manners and misconduct generally. It even includes road rage. Increasingly, recruits to our military have to be forgiven for previous confrontations with the law involving drugs, theft, sexual assault, and other misdemeanors. Without such flexibility, recruitment goals could not be met unless we reestablished a military draft.

Could such negative changes have been abetted by bad parenting and a diminishment of group relationships of the type engendered by after school activities and the formation of lasting childhood friendships that result? Certainly, they can be further abetted by television, which has been described as "sitting in your living room watching people whom you would never invite into your living room", a description that seems true quite often. As mentioned earlier, another social change that has had a severe negative impact on our children is the common financial need for both parents to work, which often leaves the children poorly supervised and lacking, in large portion, the parental interchange that results from one parent being at home with them during the day.

Several years ago, I heard a sermon by Rabbi Charles Sherman, the rabbi of Temple Israel in Tulsa, Oklahoma, on the subject of "derech eretz". He defined "derech eretz" as uncommon decency that includes civility, politeness, courtesy, good manners, and pleasant decorum toward and regard for the feelings of others. He related many poignant examples, one of which I remember well:

In 1948, the Cincinnati Reds were hosting the Brooklyn Dodgers at the time when Jackie Robinson, an African-American, was breaking the color barrier that had previously existed in major league baseball. Jackie Robinson's appearance caused a loud chorus of boos, taunts, and vile curses. As you can imagine, Robinson felt pitifully isolated not only from the crowd but even from many of his teammates. One teammate, the very popular shortstop Pee Wee Reese, felt Robinson's loneliness and abasement deeply and walked across the diamond and put his arm around the first baseman's shoulder—a profound act of "derech eretz". Reese and Robinson looked at each other with caring regard and the crowd quieted. This act of goodness by Reese may have been what it took for baseball fans everywhere to at least become tolerant of the sport becoming integrated.

Just as hate needs to be taught, so goodness needs to be taught, by words and example. Such teaching is most beneficial when transmitted early in life by good parents. For this reason, good parenting needs to be addressed much more effectively than is now the case.

As is the case with all languages, they each have words or expressions that are almost impossible to translate into any other language. So it seems with "derech eretz", which has such broad implications. This is demonstrated by another of Rabbi Sherman's examples, which he said was a true story:

A young woman got onto an elevator on which a Sam Proctor, a minister, was riding. As was his custom, Dr. Proctor tipped his hat to her. The woman became irritated by this. She said to him, "Why are you tipping your hat to me? I'm just as good as you are, and I think it's patronizing, demeaning and insulting for you to tip your hat to me". Dr. Proctor replied, "Well, ma'am, if you really want to know why I did that, I'll tell you, but we'll have to get out of the elevator if you want to know, because it will take me a couple of minutes.

They got off the elevator and he said, "I wanted you to know that if a man got into this elevator and was unfriendly to you, he would have to deal with me. I wanted you to know that if this elevator got stuck between floors, even though I know how to climb out, I wouldn't do that until I got you out first. I also wanted you to know that if you got sick in this elevator, I wouldn't get off at my floor, but I'd stay with you until you got help. Frankly, ma'am, it would have taken too long to say all that when you got on, so I just tipped my hat".

That expression of chivalry may seem a bit exaggerated as an example of "derech eretz", but the tipping of a hat used to imply comprehensive friendly regard by a man for the opposite sex – cordiality, if you will. It is almost a forgotten friendly gesture, as is the stepping aside or hold-ing a door open for a woman. For a teacher to show even the most innocent form of affection for a young child is now considered sacrilege because there are so many child predators.

All of the foregoing behavioral changes are evidence of our declining level of civility and cordiality. These declines, in their own ways, also contribute to chaotic influences.

Section IV

Biological and Atmospheric Changes Can Be Uncontrollably Regressive

Introduction

Those who are serious about the environment are referred to as "environmentalists". To many this is a derogatory reference. Although environmentalists do sometimes lose perspective with their "damn the torpedoes, full speed ahead" attitude, we had all better become more sensitive to biological change, even that which occurs naturally, and the long-term importance of protecting our environment. The cost of doing so now is relatively small compared to what it could be if neglected too long. Although environmental changes do have natural causes, there are also many causal components that derive from our misuse of nature's bounty.

I discuss only some of the environmental problems we face in this section and any environmental scientist would consider this coverage very incomplete. The purpose here is merely to make the reader aware of the seriousness of the problem.

Pollution is spoiling our planet. Unchecked, it will soon have a marked effect on our health and lifestyle. It is already contributing to the extermination of many species of plant and animal life. It is vital that we have a global effort to educate people about the environment and establish a team effort to protect the oceans, the atmosphere, our land, and fresh water resources. Yes, we have many organizations that are conscientiously addressing environmental issues, but they are not sufficiently effective in "stemming the tide". Doing a credible job will require a stronger effort by the United Nations and support by all member countries.

To put this thinking in better perspective, a review of these issues follows.

12. Pollution – The Oceans, The Atmosphere, and Water

The Oceans

The Jacques Cousteau Society is the preeminent oceanographic research organization in the world today. Its observations of decay in our oceans and the probable long-term effects on our quality of life should be taken seriously. Most of us have little understanding of our dependence on the oceans, not only for the food and minerals they provide but, more important, for the continued existence of life on our planet.

Two-thirds of the world's surface is covered by water. As former astronaut John Glenn has said, "Nowhere does this fact become more obvious, and more overwhelming, than from space. This is something that has impressed every astronaut who has gone up." According to the late Cousteau, a biological exchange is constantly occurring between the earth's atmosphere and the oceans at the surface of the seas wherever not prevented by pollution. There already are many areas of water where surface pollution prevents this biological exchange from occurring, and without this exchange the world cannot exist for long. Here we have yet another source of chaos about which the world seems oblivious.

Our rivers are the sources of most pollution that reaches our oceans. The pollution that is directly deposited by or from ocean going vessels or by humans while enjoying beaches along our shoreline is certainly important but considerably less so than that conveyed to the oceans by rivers. The pollution of rivers mostly results from manu-facturing plants dumping their wastes into rivers. Early in our history, it was common for manufacturers to purposely locate along a river. One of the many reasons for doing so was the convenience offered by the river for disposal of wastes. Many man-made lakes are polluted by rivers which flow into them. And chicken farms located on such rivers often become sources of pollution. The well-known resort beaches along the Mediterranean are so polluted as to be uninviting to bathe in. This is also true along our United States coastline in many places.

Seventy-five years ago ocean bathing was commonly enjoyed along most of our coastline without much worry about sharks. Shark attacks in shallow ocean water were very rare. Today shark attacks occur often enough to make many people afraid to swim in the ocean. Is this change due in part to the pollution of our oceans?

Many positive changes are being made in the opera-tion of oceangoing vessels. There are recognized, enforced rules that prevent the disposal of wastes into the sea. Large oil spills are being minimized and will perhaps be eliminated by the requirement that oil tankers be double-hulled so that exterior damage to the hull would be un-likely to permit the escape of oil.

Other evidence of oceanic pollution is the near-disap-pearance of many types of fish and ocean mammals such as whales. Yes, this sometimes is caused by the fishing in-dustry over-fishing some species in some locations. The refusal of some countries to limit their fishing of endangered species has caused a severe decline in their numbers.

The Atmosphere

The air to which we are exposed must not only be sufficiently clean to be healthy to breathe, but it must also contain healthy levels of chemical components such as ozone. Further, integrated over the earth's surface, the average temperature of the earth's atmosphere must stay within certain limits so as not to cause us another ice age or severe melting of the polar ice cap. Any long-term exception to these limitations surely will cause us atmospheric chaos, although in this context long-term may be decades.

We are well-acquainted with the problems of urban smog and excessive ozone and are taking steps to control them. Such problems are acute in California, so it is not surprising that California leads the nation in applying controls to limit the adverse effects of automobiles and industry on the atmosphere. The same problems are being faced in most urban areas; even such inland cities as Denver, Tulsa, and Phoenix, where you would expect the cleanest air, have needed to take preventive measures. Industry is gradually taking the necessary steps to cease being a source of pollution, but many utilities and basic type industries such as refineries and steel plants have a long way to go. They know of the problems and are addressing them, but the speed with which progress is being made is often intentionally kept to a snail's pace in deference to the "bottom line". Certainly we cannot expect any business to jeopardize its existence by spending for pollution control faster than its financial strength permits, but government must find ways to help in such circumstances. Tax incentives or low-interest loans should be made available as necessary.

Most air pollution results from our consumption of fuel in its many forms. Be it wood, coal, petroleum products, or atomic energy, all are, or can be, sources of air pollution, if proper technology is not applied. Proper technology includes such devices as smokestack scrubbers, which minimize pollutants that otherwise would be vented into the atmosphere from an industrial chimney, and catalytic converters, which reduce automobile exhaust emissions; it also includes recycling exhaust gases, maintaining an ideal fuel/air mix, maintaining ideal combustion temperatures, and many other factors. Although continuing progress is being made in improving the efficiency of fuel consumption, old technology of lesser efficiency is often phased out over too extended a time span. An article in the World Street Journal of December 14, 2007 reports that geochemists chart carbon dioxide levels at concentrations not seen in 650,000 years. Not only are we putting more carbon dioxide into the atmosphere than ever before, but our overall ecosystem is not operating as effectively as it did years ago. The oceans, plant life and soil have all historically absorbed much of the carbon dioxide emitted into the atmosphere, but, as reported in this article, the ability of such natural "sponges" to absorb our spills of carbon dioxide has steadily declined. Additional discussion on the subject of energy follows.

Pollution may be responsible for the appreciable reduction in the bee population, a problem with potentially serious consequences for our overall agricultural well-being, although the precise cause has not been identified as of this writing. We depend on bees to cross-pollinate many types of plants and trees. A recent headline on CNN indicated a possible negative economic impact of billions of dollars because of the disease affecting a bee, which is referred to as colony collapse disorder.

We are aware that soil can be so seriously depleted of nutrients within a few years as to be unfit to grow foodstuff. To prevent this, farmers regularly rotate crops and fertilize their land. Unfortunately, they typically add to the soil only what is needed to enhance the volume and salability of their crops, not to replace most of the missing nutrients which might make for healthier foods.

Many of our medical ills seem more prevalent today than was the case decades ago, in spite of the tremendous advances made by medical science. These ills include allergies, diabetes, cancer, digestive difficulties, and mental illness. There are those who say that this is the case because we are better able to detect and report such illnesses. Certainly there has been much progress by the medical profession, including drug manufacturers, in their ability to lessen the severity and discomfort such ailments cause us, and a greater percentage of cancer patients are surviving past five years from the date of original diagnosis.

Sometime in 2008, while traveling, I read an article in U.S.A Today which stated that in 1904 cancer was almost unheard of. I failed to save the article and have been unable therefore to document it properly. In trying to document it, using the internet, I have observed so many references to the year 1904 that you might surmise that that year was the first significant year in which medical statistics were accumulated. I have discussed with several elder citizens, who are mentally alert and able to respond with meaningful recollections, the prevalence of disease seventy or more years ago. There seems to be consensus that among their family and friends they were unaware of diseases such as cancer, polio, and Alzheimer back then. Of course polio has been virtually eliminated since that time by the Salk vaccine. They also agreed that several diseases such as diphtheria, scarlet fever, tuberculosis, and erysipelas are very rare today. The latter changes result from the development of immunization vaccines, timely control of infection with antibiotics, and substantial over-all improvement in hygiene related practices. In spite of these significant advances, we no longer rank among the top few countries in terms of longevity or the survival rates of newborns. An article in the Tulsa World entitled *"Life expectancy in U.S. being surpassed"* notes claims made by Dr. Christopher Murray, head of The Institute for Health Metrics and Evaluation at the University of Washington. Dr. Murray indicates that although a baby born in the United States in 2004 will live an average of 77.9 years, that life expectancy ranks 42nd, down from 11th two decades earlier. The article also states that forty countries, including Cuba, Taiwan, and most of Europe, have lower infant mortality rates than the United States in 2004. After discussing these issues with practicing physicians, I have come to believe that lack of medical insurance or access to proper medical care is largely the cause. One of those physicians referred to such conditions as "a disaster of our society". In the same Tulsa World article reference is also made to the fact that infant mortality among African-American Americans was twice that of our average rate which gives credence to the opinions I received from practicing physicians.

An article by Kathleen Parker of *The Washington Post* reports a recent downward trend in the percentages of males born, not only in the United States but also in other parts of the world. In both the United States and Japan, between 1970 and 2001, the drop was approximately one percent. In the United States, that drop was from 105.5 to 104.6 males to every 100 females. Although that dip is small, researchers at the University of Pittsburgh believe that environmental pollution is taking a toll on the male reproductive system. There has been confirming data gathered in Italy from men who were exposed to dioxin from an industrial accident. They fathered significantly fewer boys than girls. This information adds further evidence of the apparent ill effect that a polluted environment has on humankind. In the January 4th, 2009 issue of the *Internet Journal of Urology* Shiva Dindyai, of the Imperial College School of Medicine in the United Kingdom, is quoted as follows: "If the decrease in sperm counts were to continue at the present rate in a few years we will witness widespread male infertility". He questions whether there is an endocrine basis for this decrease which indicates that he and his fellow researchers are unsure of the cause. They speculate that the cause could be our atmospheric environment.

If the foregoing circumstantial evidence about some diseases not having been prevalent early in the 1900s is added to the decline in both the birth rate of males and the decrease in sperm count, do we have an overall long-term negative trend to worry about? Researchers at the

University of Pittsburgh also refer to the apparent ill effect the environment is having on humankind. Similar comments have been made by environmentalists with regard to carbon emissions into the atmosphere. If an exhaustive study were made of any such possible trend, in my opinion, it also should include the possible need for basic revisions to our diet and lifestyle as suggested by Topic 13, "Soil Erosion and The Hunzas".

Water

Ismail Serageldin, a former vice-president of the World Bank, in his book *Managing Water Resources* states that we are headed toward a serious world water crisis. He indicates that eighty countries are already experiencing water shortages which threaten agricultural production, and notes that with an anticipated 40 percent increase in population over the next thirty years the situation will become critical unless an effective water conservation program is adopted soon.

At the present time, fresh water usage is almost doubling globally every twenty years. In poorer countries, where most available water is used for irrigation, because water is sprayed over a wide area of crops, much of it evaporates and is therefore largely wasted. Only a small percentage of it actually reaches the crops. Water used for bathing or laundry is often from a nearby but contaminated stream. Clean, municipally provided water is unusual. This combination of factors is responsible for much disease. The sad fact is that there are existing techniques which would help in most areas of the world were they put into practice. For example, in Israel, where water is in very short supply, "drip irrigation" channels virtually all the water directly to the crops. This is done by distributing water through plastic pipes containing small holes that allow water to drip right onto the soil beneath a plant's foliage. The water is thus delivered only as fast as the soil can absorb it, and evaporation is minimized.

The Rocky Mountain Institute, a nonprofit organization located in Colorado, is devoted to research and education in the field of energy and water conservation. Its scientists have developed shower heads and toilet-flushing systems that reduce water consumption over 50 percent. Their flushing systems did not function well at first, but they have been improved considerably and are still being improved. It is important that the world adopt such conservation methods as soon as possible. Change takes time, but we do not have much time before it will be too late.

In agriculture, organic farming practitioners have shown that biologically sound production methods will build soil fertility and production will take care of itself without the use of chemicals. Although agricultural chemicals and pesticides have permitted rapid growth and productivity, they also have negative long-term side effects for both the soil and the nutritional value of the foods grown. We have heard of soil being depleted and no longer good for farming. These long-term side effects may be responsible for aggravating many of our ills and costing us more in health care than is saved in the farming process. We are depleting not only our soil but our bodies as well. Such thinking becomes particularly germane when our government is urgently trying to reduce the cost of healthcare. We spend huge sums of money for medical treatment of the elderly and the indigent. Were a few million spent developing new, efficient methods of organic farming there could be an exponential payback in reduced medical costs. It would certainly be better to spend for prevention, rather than treatment, of disease. We should refer such thinking to an unbiased, qualified think tank - not to prove that such thinking makes sense but to convince our government to act on disease prevention.

There has been such a marked increase in demand for organically grown foods that there is a considerable increase of interest in organic farming. As a result, we can probably expect much progress in the application of mechanized farming methods to organic farming. This will reduce the seeming gap in savings that results from the pervasive use of chemicals and pesticides.

A close friend, recently returned from a trip to Turkey, reports that the fruit and vegetables there tasted surprisingly better that those sold by our domestic supermarkets. The apparent reason is that labor in Turkey is relatively cheap and, therefore, farming is closer to being organic in nature. And perhaps those foods were permitted a greater level of ripening on the vine.

Were we to truly appreciate the world's vast supply of minerals and energy resources, realizing that they are largely irreplaceable, we might use them more conservatively in consideration of future generations. Although we tend to think of them as inventory that flows from an endless supply, it would be more appropriate to regard them as "nature's capital", which we continue to use without giving thought to replenishment.

With increasing frequency, municipal water treatment processes fail to provide healthy drinking water. As in so many other areas of nature, microscopic waterborne bacteria, parasites, and viruses are turning deadly, forcing health departments to shift priorities as they try to make drinking water safe. According to the Environmental Protection Agency, some bacteria such as cryptosporidium and girardiasis were largely unknown or ignored until a few years ago. New York City found that their aging water piping system contained many bacteria in spite of the usual application of chlorine. They are in the process of correcting this condition but still have a way to go. I have read that Washington D.C. has a problem similar to New York City, with people hesitant to drink the city water.

The Center for Disease Control and Prevention in Atlanta estimates that close to one thousand people die each year due to microbial illnesses contracted from drinking water. Unfortunately, susceptibility to such illness is highest among our elderly and those suffering from immune systems weakened by infection or diseases such as AIDS or cancer. The necessary upgrading of our water purification systems is usually so costly as to suffer constant delay, but in most cities the need exists. In addition to the foregoing problems, we have only recently become aware that seepage of plastics into our municipal water systems will require changes in either our waste disposal systems or our water purification processes. Apparently too much plastic waste is improperly discarded as trash instead of being recycled.

13. Soil Depletion and the Hunzas

With our agricultural soil being depleted constantly, about the only places that have the quality of virgin farm soil are on, or at the bases of, mountains. Most of our arable soil lacks soluble minerals and salts. This is so because as rainwater filters though topsoil it tends to absorb available soluble minerals and salts subsequently carrying much of that material with it into our rivers and then into the oceans. This process has been going on for eons and largely accounts for the saltiness of oceans. With evaporation from water surfaces of all kinds there is appreciable recirculation of water and redistribution via rains, but such redistribution is not so complete as to eliminate severe water shortages, as we know. Also, in the imperfect redistribution of water, because minerals do not evaporate to any appreciable degree, they remain in the ocean. When our agricultural industry finally recognizes and addresses this phenomenon properly, we will enjoy much healthier food and probably a huge reduction in medical expenses. Because such change will not improve profits for the drug industry, and because the medical profession is largely uneducated in the field of nutrition, it is probably years away.

There are places in our world where many of the diseases from which we suffer are not prevalent. Most of them are at the bases of large mountains, where rainwater reaches the bottom of the mountain and leaves there an appreciable quantity of minerals it has taken from the surface of the mountain. Because of the relatively huge mass of earth contained in the mountain, the soluble salts and minerals are still plentiful.

Within the Himalaya mountain range, in Northwest Pakistan, there is place called Hunza, a tiny country almost hidden in the mountain passes of that area. If with Google (on your computer) you access the subject of Hunza, you will find an essay by Jane Kinderlehrer entitled "Death Rides a Slow Bus in Hunza". She alludes to "a slow bus" in consideration of the tranquil and lengthy lives lived there. She refers to it as "a land where cancer has not yet been invented, a land where an optometrist discovers to his amazement that everyone has perfect 20-20 vision, a land where cardiologists cannot find a trace of coronary heart disease, and a land without ulcers, appendicitis or gout". People there live vigorous lives past the age of 100 years and enjoy average longevity well past the age of 120. At age 100, they run up and down mountains and are sexually active. They live at an altitude of 6,000 to 9,000 feet (approximately the altitude of Vail, Colorado or Santa Fe, New Mexico) and the pure drinking water they use trickles down from glaciers much higher. They have no need for drugs or chemicals such as we use in fertilizers.

Their lifestyle is very spartan and virtually without any of the luxuries of civilization. Behavior patterns there are without crime, as we know it, and hence there are no jails. Also, there are no reports of mental illness. I wonder what might be observed were one of our bigger prisons used for a test in which all employees and inmates were provided with a diet and supplements to raise their mineral and nutritional salt levels up to that of the Hunzas, which may differ from what we have heretofore considered ideal. The resulting behavioral changes might be surprisingly improved.

The lifestyle and dietary habits of the Hunzas have been studied and restudied numerous times without arriving at definitive reasons for their extremely good health. Yes, their diet is ideal, consisting of fruits, vegetables, beans, nuts, seeds, and only one percent animal products. But, apparently emulating such habits in other parts of the world does not come close to achieving the level of physical well being and longevity they enjoy, although it does improve health considerably.

The average precipitation in Hunza is less than two inches per year. The valley in which they live was originally bare rock. The soil in which their foodstuffs are grown is contained within hand-crafted terraces in which the soil is continually replaced, by hand, with new soil obtained from the Hunza River, 3,000 feet below. Therein seems to lay the principal reason for the good health enjoyed by the Hunzas. That soil is extremely rich in minerals and natural salts. This seems to substantiate the claim that the best sources of minerals and salts important to our bodies are found on or at the bases of mountains, an observation seemingly neglected by the many previous investigations into their lifestyle. Because the Hunzas constantly replace the soil in which their foodstuffs are grown with soil that has the nutrient giving quality of virgin soil, they have no need for crop rotation or fertilizers.

Many other tribes that live at the base of the Andes in South America also enjoy good health, comparable to the

Hunzas, and there are numerous instances of middle-aged people with degenerative diseases who achieve cures after living with such tribes for several months but again become sick after returning home. A long list of Andean tribes that enjoy unusually good health can also be accessed using a search engine on your computer.

Because we could not adapt to such a spartan lifestyle, devoid of the luxuries we are accustomed to, it is unlikely that anything we might learn from the Hunzas would permit us the level of health they enjoy; but merely providing our bodies with the high level of minerals and salts they obtain from the food they consume might be of immense benefit in reducing the huge cost of medicine in the United States If we did that, made our farming more organic, and drank pure water (as they do), we might enjoy most of the good health benefits they experience! Although such change would have to occur slowly, eventually a significant reduction in our annual federal budget should result!

Many years ago, our United States Department of Health determined that we tended to be short of iodine. Although the cause was not evident, they decided to add iodine to our table salt to eliminate that deficiency. Because iodine is highly soluble, it was probably one of the first nutrients to have found its way into the oceans. Of course, we consume salt in varying degrees, and now that salt is regarded as something we should minimize in our food since it can have a negative impact on our circulatory system, iodine shortage may again rear its ugly head. Perhaps people who really minimize salt usage would be wise to consume a few kelp tablets each week, since kelp comes from the oceans and contains appreciable iodine. The use of salt tablets to compensate for the loss of electrolytes caused by sweating due to exercise or exposure to high atmospheric temperatures very often proves to have negative results because sodium chloride is but one of the many electrolytes we lose with perspiration. A good electrolyte fluid is considered preferable. This commentary about salt is included here only as further evidence about the depletion of soluble salts in our soil.

Although there is a gradually increasing trend toward organic farming, which does address the replenishment of soil nutrients and/or minerals, the resulting benefits accrue mostly to those who can afford the greater cost of organic foods. Many doctors still advise their patients that organic foods are largely a "rip-off" and we should obtain adequate nutrition from virtually any average diet. Of course, such opinions reflect the direct or indirect influence of the drug companies whose influence on medical schools seems to have minimized nutritional training available to medical students. Somehow, the change to organic farming should be supported by government in the interest of the people. Perhaps when drug company executives care as much about the health of their grandchildren as they do for their company's bottom line, they too may support such change. Yes, drug companies must make profits, but it should be possible to do so and still operate a little closer to the Golden Rule.

The foregoing commentary on soil depletion and the Hunzas does not seem, on the surface, to contribute directly to any chaotic trend. It can contribute, long-term and in a major way, to our nation's increasing cost of health insurance and Medicare, which has become very high. Further, the conclusions reached, if valid, suggest that if our diets provided ideal levels of minerals and salts we would enjoy much better health, improved longevity, and a major reduction in debilitating disease. Such increasing costs are a sizeable factor in our extreme national debt which is trending toward chaos.

We all know of people who, in their eating habits, have become vegetarians, vegans, or mainly consumers of only raw foods. Others avoid sugar or carbohydrates. Some pay strict attention to a glycemic index. Some eat their big meal earlier in the day and eat a very light meal at dinner time. Although adherents to such eating patterns usually do improve their overall health, they still fail to come close to the level of good health and longevity enjoyed by the Hunzas. These ways of eating seem to me to overlook the reason for the oceans being so salty. That observation is, perhaps, even further evidence of the need for investigation of this phenomenon.

If you have been impressed with this essay on "Soil Depletion and The Hunzas", and wonder how you can implement a beneficial change in your lifestyle as a result, you may be interested in how we have done it in my family. We use double distilled water to which we add liquid minerals that are available in any health food store. We now add about 30 percent more than what is suggested by the manufacturer. The amount needed to reach the high level of minerals in the bodies of the Hunzas is really unknown. As with so many things, too much can be toxic, for which reason I have stepped up the amount of liquid minerals added to our water very slightly about twice a year after first starting with what is recommended. Further, when we travel, we use mineral tablets made by the same manufacturer. It was of interest to me to observe the description and usage recommendations on the label which says: "Trace minerals provide full spectrum, body balanced minerals from 'ConcenTrace' and are designed to replace trace minerals commonly found deficient in today's diet. You may expect a wide spectrum of nutritional benefits". Under suggested usage, it says: "For regular use, take 1-3 tablets daily. Moderately increased dosages are safe if needed or desired but larger amounts may have a laxative effect". Thus far, my increasing the amount of minerals we have been consuming has not had a laxative effect. Further, in spite of my living most of my life without adherence to the health concepts I now espouse, these changes still seem to be benefiting me.

In all the foregoing commentary relative to the possible shortage of minerals in our foods, please be aware that even though my conclusions seem to be based on convincing observations, they have not yet been investigated by our National Institute of Health which might require a lengthy double blind study. Also, I certainly am not a medical professional and do not recommend your making any changes in your diet unless based on your own reasoning or on recommendations from a medical professional.

14. Energy

The consumption of energy particularly that which derives from fossil fuels is vastly higher per capita in the United States than in any other country. Yes, energy contributes to a higher standard of living, but the manner in which we use it also has a negative impact on our standard of living. Pollution is a continuous source of danger to our health. Fighting it, at great expense, has had but limited effectiveness, since our consumption of fossil fuels seems to rise constantly. All we have been able to accomplish so far is to reduce the rate of growth in our usage of fossil fuels. With increasing frequency, power outages cause shutdowns of all regional activity that depends on electrical power except those that have emergency backup power sources.

Our dependency on foreign sources for an increasing percentage of the oil we consume, now well over 50 percent, puts us at risk in the event of international conflict. It is another potential path toward chaos that we need to eliminate. Reducing our dependency on foreign sources for petroleum would be less difficult if we would attack the problem in a rational way. Even if the availability of oil from foreign sources continues without interruption of a political nature, these foreign sources and oil reserves yet undiscovered will ultimately dry up as we consume nature's irreplaceable assets. Although such guesses have proven incorrect in the past, perhaps with greater accuracy, petroleum geologists say that worldwide petroleum reserves are now declining relative to new discoveries at an ever-increasing rate.

The Rocky Mountain Institute has done considerable work in the area of fuel conservation. Staff have designed buildings that are not prone to inside air contamination, which are heated in the winter by the heat thrown off from appliances (toasters, coffeepots, cooking stoves, electric lights), and cooled with a minimum of air conditioning during the summer. Inside air is refreshed by a constant infusion of outside air and exhausting of stale inside air through heat exchanger devices that recover about 80 percent of the energy that might otherwise be lost in the process. They have developed design approaches that could decrease the fuel consumption of automobiles substantially by the recovery of energy when the vehicle is going downhill and by streamlining the undercarriage. Many of their findings with regard to automobiles are currently being applied by automobile manufacturers. Such conservation usually increases initial vehicle cost, but fuel savings more than make up for that in a reasonable time. Were all known and practical conservation methods applied, we would not be nearly so dependent on foreign sources for most of our petroleum.

A speaker at a meeting sponsored by the University of Tulsa Foreign Relations Committee in the late 1970's went so far as to conclude that proper conservation policies could eliminate our dependency on foreign crude oil without lowering our standard of living.

Perhaps the cleanest energy source is atomic energy, but until we find a way of suitably disposing of atomic wastes and preventing atomic contamination, the generation of electricity by this method has many drawbacks. Since its problems may be solved satisfactorily one day, perhaps there is justification for continuing research and development in that area. What occurred at Chernobyl in the former Soviet Union when they suffered a severe atomic accident is evidence of how disastrous an atomic accident can be. The nuclear contamination from that accident spread around the world and may have been responsible for much ill-health. The absorption by nature of such contamination to levels that are no longer dangerous takes decades.

Congress is now proposing to require automobiles sold in the United States after 2020 to obtain mileage of 30 to 35 miles per gallon. This is a positive step, no doubt, but because the number of miles driven in our country is on the rise, it will probably prove to be insufficient and too late in its effect.

Canada has huge deposits of what are referred to as Athabaska Tar Sands that contain large volumes of oil that can be recovered at a relatively high cost. As the price of oil has escalated, that cost has become economically viable, and although oil is increasingly produced from this source, it will be several years before these tar sands become a major source such as we find in the Middle East. Also, in Colorado, much oil is recoverable from oil shale, but there they have a severe problem disposing of the waste residues without leaving severe contamination behind. That problem will probably will be solved, and these two sources of oil have the possibility of largely reducing our dependence on foreign sources.

There are many other positive efforts that are reducing our consumption of energy. These include development of the hydrogen fuel cell, an improved version of electrically powered cars whose batteries can be charged from a home electrical outlet, buses that reduce idling time by using electronic equipment that changes traffic lights to green upon approach, and traffic control patterns to reduce the idling time of passenger cars. Unfortunately, all such efforts, although positive in their results, are not sufficient to get the job done. Any political upset in the Middle East could be a major source of chaos in a very short time because worldwide consumption of oil is on the rise. As has been shown prior to our present financial reversal, when oil production exceeds consumption by but a small margin, even the impact of a hurricane on offshore oil rigs causes the price of oil to rise.

The United States is very much more energy-efficient today than it was a few decades ago, however. That is due to more fuel-efficient cars and appliances of all kinds and improved building standards. We are also beginning to utilize light bulbs that are much more energy-efficient. Unfortunately, these changes are occurring too slowly. A program that would encourage bringing older homes up to current fuel efficiency standards would help immensely.

15. Disappearing Species and Killer Bugs

A report originating from a global biodiversity assessment by the United Nations of the world's fading diversity says that humankind is destroying animal and plant species at an alarming rate. That report was released in November of 1995 at an international conference in Jakarta, Indonesia. The statistics cited are difficult for most of us to put in perspective, but they estimate that there are over thirteen million species, of which over thirty thousand are threatened with extinction. Since less than two million species have been formally identified, the probability is that the number being threatened is much higher.

The long-term importance of such information is given credence by an example the author cites of a species of day-flying moth that is found in South America and Mexico. Before reading further, you might think, *so what?* However, that moth metamorphoses from a caterpillar that feeds exclusively on a variety of trees and vines known as omphalea. The leaves of those trees and vines are being eaten so profusely by the caterpillars that nature is causing the leaves to produce a chemical toxin that repels the moths. This toxic plant compound has been shown to be effective against the AIDS virus in laboratory experiments. The toxin is produced only by the interaction between these species of moths and plants, which are dying out because of the gradual disappearance of the leaves. If this seeming magical product of nature becomes unavailable, we may regret our not having tried to reverse its destruction.

Although the foregoing example of the gradual disappearance of a species is not the result of what we consider environmental negligence, it points to the need to protect nature by reducing the destruction of species wherever we can reasonably do so. It is rash to assume that any species is unimportant to humankind, even those whose proliferation we cannot control.

Environmentalists not only worry about protecting virtually every species of animal and plant life from harm but often do so without justifying the cost. Most of us scoff at the need to prevent the extinction of seemingly undesirable and pesky insects, plants that we regard as weeds or birds that seem to be of no benefit to society. Too often the cost for such protection does seem excessive and beyond the understanding of us tax payers.

Biologists will confirm that there is deep interdependency among all the elements of nature, for which reason we must be extremely careful to prevent the inadvertent extinction of species. Unknown to the public at large, however, thousands of species have already disappeared, and large numbers will disappear in the future, regardless of how careful we are. At the time of this writing, rainbow trout are rapidly decreasing in numbers in eleven states, and the guilty parasite has been identified in at least nine others. It is thought that the parasite was accidentally imported from Europe where, through the ages, the brown trout had developed immunity to it. Here in the United States, if the rainbow trout does not develop such immunity, it will soon disappear as a species. Whether this problem could have been prevented is unknown, and whether the demise of rainbow trout as a species would have any long-term impact on our well-being is also unknown. It is only recently that fish biologists have begun to study this particular problem, which could prove to be more serious if the parasite were to affect other fish species as well.

It is also true that were all plant and animal species classified as to their potential future importance to humankind, there would be many that would rate very low on the list. It would probably be unwise to regard the disappearance of any species as a normal part of the process of evolution, however. For example, doing so might result in our overlooking changes that we should make in our regard for the environment that could prevent the demise of the rainbow trout.

Several years ago, the bald eagle was decreasing in numbers so rapidly that, under the Endangered Species Act, it was put on a protected list. This made it a misdemeanor to harm one. As reported in *The Wall Street Journal,* a privately-funded group of conservationists initiated a project in which a significant number of bald eagles were confined in a controlled area and permitted to propagate over an extended period of time. Assuming that these efforts would be successful, at some future date they would release the increased number from the confined area. So that the eagles would not have become domesticated as a result of being fed and otherwise cared for by humans, those who were responsible for such care even wore camouflage suits. In mid-2007, the project was deemed a success and the birds were taken off the endangered species list. The cost of that project was approximately $4,000 per bird. Those involved felt the project was worth the cost and say it is further evidence that the Endangered Species Act is working.

The National Audubon Society tracks numerous bird species and observes that twenty bird populations have declined over 50 percent. Carol Browner, their chairman and former head of the United States Environmental Protection Agency calls such declines "a warning signal". They are concerns, and, as she says, "concerns can quickly become emergencies".

Gerard C. Armas of The Associated Press reported in June of 2007 that honeybee colonies have been dying out at an alarming rate from an unknown cause. Because fruit growers and farmers depend on bees to pollinate more than ninety types of flowering crops, including apples, nuts, and citrus trees, bees are vital to our food supply, another potential serious problem.

At the same time that some species are disappearing, we can observe the increased vitality of other species, a few being both virulent and severely infectious. These observations are primarily in the field of medicine, where some bacterial forms are becoming resistant to antibiotics, causing considerable apprehension for doctors. The death rate from infectious diseases increased an astonishing 58 percent between 1980 and 1992 and is, no doubt, still on the rise. Although much of that rise was due to the AIDS virus, increases due to other diseases were high also.

AIDS was unheard of a several decades ago. Who knows but what it is caused by an infectious source that mutated from some other type of infection source? We now know of a new disease in which a patient's flesh is actually consumed by an infection source. It can certainly be referred to as a "killer bug", since it does cause death in a high percentage of affected people.

As the percentage of our population over the age of sixty-five increases, there has also been an expected increase in respiratory tract infections that doctors traditionally treat with antibiotics. Tuberculosis is rapidly becoming drug-resistant, but the medical community at large seems to make light of it probably because it is not yet widespread. Incidence of antibiotics not working as expected being a problem is already becoming common in Europe as reported by the World Health Organization. In Columbus, Ohio, several years ago, doctors became alarmed when 14 percent of patients with a dangerous form of pneumonia did not respond to what was then the antibiotic of choice. The Centers for Disease Control and Prevention is aggressively addressing this growing problem, but overall the problem is aggravated by excessive use of antibiotics. Such excessive use results not only from the desire of medical practitioners to be effective, but from patients persuading doctors to prescribe antibiotics – even for colds, which do not respond to them. Obviously, the more we use antibiotics, the sooner infectious bugs will become resistant to them. They are then referred to as "killer bugs".

16. Natural Disasters

Earthquakes, floods, forest and widespread suburban fires, tornadoes, and droughts have impacted various regions of our country so severely during the past few years that insurance companies have found themselves underfinanced to cope with the resulting claims.

Weather records of over 100 years' standing have been broken. It may soon be necessary for many building codes, such as those that depend on an assumed depth of frost line or the definition of a flood plain, to be revised. All such codes are based on experience that is now being violated by the forces of nature.

The expert city planners of cities such as Mexico City, Tokyo, San Francisco, and Los Angeles must update their thinking based on recently observed earthquake data. The building code revisions to come will create unplanned expenses for new construction and possible reductions in value for older buildings that cannot comply easily. In the case of California, there is evidence of appreciable migration of people to neighboring states to escape the prevalence of natural disasters they have experienced on the West Coast. The price to pay for enjoying California's usually pleasant weather has become excessive for them.

In 1993, the drought in Southern California had lasted so long that water usage had to be severely restricted. Car washing, lawn and shrub watering, baths, and even toilet use were all restricted in varying degrees, with penalties applying to observed noncompliance. I was told there by relatives at whose home I was a guest, "If it's yellow, let it mellow; if it's brown, flush it down". Their yard was severely sun-scorched and probably required much work and expense to restore. Many home owners suffered foundation damage cause by unusually dry sub-soil.

In 2007, England suffered severe flooding due to rains that rivaled the biblical "forty days and forty nights". Rains even flooded a major power plant, leaving a large, populated area without power. With global warming now evident and 100-year records being broken with regard to temperature extremes, drought, flooding, uncontrolled fires, and hurricanes, we are certainly suffering from an increase in natural disasters. We can do little to prevent them. Instead, we must concentrate our efforts on improving our preparedness and our responses to minimize discomfort and loss of life.

A recent advertisement by the American Insurance Association graphically presented the ten most expensive natural disasters in recent history. The oldest was Hurricane Hugo in 1989, which cost $7.43 billion; the latest was Hurricane Wilma, which cost $12.9 billion. The most expensive was Hurricane Katrina, which cost $66.31 billion. The total cost of all ten disasters was $191 billion. It is certainly difficult for an insurance company to plan for such disasters and price them into the policies they sell, and it is financially nearly impossible for them to entirely satisfy their customers under such chaotic circumstances. They have gradually revised their policies to reduce the liability extremes to which they have previously been subjected. Some companies have even refused to write insurance in areas prone to natural disasters. Public opinion and even government seem to take an anti-insurance company attitude.

We are gradually making constructive changes that improve resistance to natural disasters. These include building restrictions such as requirements that doors and windows be strong enough to withstand 150-mile-per-hour wind conditions; that homes be built so that floor levels are above record flood levels; that roofs be more wind-resistant; and that construction levees and sea walls be improved. There is even a circular factory-built house that is designed to tolerate 150-mile-per-hour winds. Unfortunately, these changes are not widely applied and are having very little impact so far. We are still almost as ever susceptible to chaotic conditions resulting from natural disasters.

17. Global Warming and Other Atmospheric Changes

Is the earth's atmosphere warming up? Are we polluting the atmosphere severely enough to destroy the ozone layer that shields us from the very strong ultraviolet rays emanating from the sun? These are subjects of much debate that has produced a wide variety of opinions. Even scientific research has produced much conflicting data. Adding to the confusion are opinions of those who arrive at desired conclusions without background, or through the inclusion of incomplete data.

However, when people living in the south of Argentina have to adapt to the increased penetration of the sun's rays, as reported in the *Coastal Post* on December 1, 1997, we had better initiate a definitive study to determine what we have to contend with in that regard and what can be done to ameliorate the harmful impact of such change. When we can observe areas where the northern ice cap is receding, a similar high-quality study must be made to determine how any resulting long-term increases in sea levels may impact our shores. Even a small rise in sea level could have a chaotic impact on our coastal cities and suburban areas. There are islands in the Pacific already suffering from the rise in sea level. In fact, New Zealand is expecting to become a haven for thousands of people needing to escape Pacific islands inundated by the rising sea level. With the northern ice cap receding, the seasonable weather available for farming in Greenland has increased appreciably, to residents' benefit. Global warming is definitely being observed in many places on our planet. Galveston, Texas is already observing a disturbing and potentially damaging rise in sea level.

Although some of our right-wing commentators insist that these changes are not occurring and should not be a cause for concern, it is comforting that the EPA has decreed that the use of Freon must be curtailed in air-conditioning equipment. The United States Environmental Protection Agency, in a report dated August 1944 indicated that Freon released into the atmosphere gradually moves slowly into the stratosphere where it causes ozone depletion. Thinning the earth's ozone layer in turn permits increased ultra violet radiation which can adversely affect human health. Yes, there is geological evidence showing that the earth has gone through warming periods before, so there is justification for presuming that humankind may not be entirely to blame for our apparent global warming problem. However, if we aggravate the problem, global warming can and will have a greater and more damaging impact on our atmosphere as a result. We should, therefore, do whatever we can to decrease the polluting emissions of carbon.

Another atmospheric problem, although local in nature, is noise. Our young people seem to be happier with sound at very high levels, considerably above the decibel level it is recommended we stay below to prevent damage to our hearing. We have all heard radios referred to as "boom boxes" turned up to such loud levels you can hear them a block away. Catering to the high percentage of our young who are so inclined, restaurants are prone to be purposely noisy, oftentimes so bad that even at a small table for four it is difficult to communicate with anyone eating with you. After eating in such an environment, you are left unrelaxed because of the noise. When asked why he did not do something about this problem, a local owner of four successful restaurants replied, "If it ain't broke, why fix it?" Perhaps he has invested in a hearing aid manufacturing company, because our younger generation is guaranteeing the financial future of hearing aid manufacturers. The percentage of our population who are regarded as senior citizens is increasing, and virtually all of them would appreciate a restaurant that offered a relaxing atmosphere without such high noise levels. While in a very noisy place one senior citizen was heard to say, "This place is noisy enough to be a restaurant".

As reported in the *New Scientist*, in November 1997, a recent study by the World Health Organization finds that long-term exposure to high noise levels poses dangerous health risks. It contributes to heart disease, and noise from daytime automobile traffic may be a factor in some deaths from heart attacks and strokes. New York has introduced laws to combat noise pollution. Anti-noise campaigners hope that eventually excessive noise will become as unacceptable as smoking.

Contrasted with the foregoing diatribe on noisy restaurants are the highly successful ongoing revisions to many of the products we use that have been annoyingly noisy. These include dishwashers, ceiling fans, garbage disposals, automobiles and many others.

Noise is a form of energy and can be expressed graphically in much the same way as is a cardiogram. If noise can be generated that produces such a graph with like frequency but opposite in phase, it cancels out the undesirable noise. Often this is referred to as "white noise". Perhaps sound engineers will one day, develop a white noise generator small enough to carry with you into a restaurant that would reduce annoying background noise. Noise cancellation techniques are having a decided impact on household appliances. Dishwashers of recent manufacture can hardly be heard, and ceiling fans are so quiet that without a red light indicating when they are on, you might very well forget to turn them off.

18. Sewage and Solid Waste

In recent years, many cities have built waste disposal plants that permit neutralizing sewage, making it non-polluting before discharging it into rivers or disposal wells. However, our streams, rivers, and lakes are still very polluted. Pollution can come from natural sources, but more often the culprit is industrial pollution resulting from improper disposal of contaminated effluents into our waterways. In their book *Water Pollution and Society* David Krantz and Brad Kefferstein effectively decry this inadequately monitored problem. There is much pressure brought to bear on those who are responsible, primarily because of the adverse effect on rivers and lakes used for recreation. The long-term effect on our oceans, to which most rivers eventually flow, is a subject that is usually overlooked.

Businesses that cannot effect sufficient savings from pollution control to amortize the cost usually do not volunteer such control. For that reason, we are seeing increasing government regulation and bureaucracy working to clean up our waterways. The overall cost of doing so would be considerably less were industry to do this without the need for legislation and compliance inspection.

Science may come to our aid in this endeavor, according to the report of a research project which has been ongoing for some time at the Massachusetts Institute of Technology. As reported in the September issue of *MIT Tech Talk*, they have been using a plasma furnace, a furnace capable of producing temperatures up to 18,000 degrees Fahrenheit, to turn toxic and municipal wastes into harmless blocks of glass. The process has been referred to as "manmade lightning". The furnace even has great potential for disposing of nuclear waste. In the latter case, the resulting blocks of glass would be radioactive, unfortunately; but, because they would be stable and not prone to leaching radioactive molecules, it would be a great step forward compared to encasing radioactive materials in cement, which is unstable in the long term. This plasma process has been known for some time, but as a result of the MIT project, it may soon become a viable and economically practical pollution-control tool.

19. Food

In 2007, we have been beset with contaminated foods imported from China. That China does not have purity standards equal to ours is not a surprise, since it is only in the last quarter-century that China has significantly progressed from being an agrarian society. The Chinese have made substantial progress in industrialization and urbanization. Their cities have grown and are spectacular to see. However, their very disappointing response to our finding fault with their foodstuffs is deserving of our most serious condemnation. The foodstuffs that have been most contaminated are toothpaste, preserved fruit, and fish. An article in *The Wall Street Journal* cites a 2007 review by the Chinese government of more than 6,300 food companies; in which they found that nearly 20 percent of them failed quality and safety standards. Hard to understand is the fact that they are apparently inspecting shipments of toothpaste to the United States more closely but continue to market the same contaminated toothpaste in China. They claim that our standards are unnecessarily strict. The fact that people may suffer illness from the use of their products seems unimportant to them.

Most often, the discovery of infectious contamination in our food is made as a result of people becoming ill. With global terrorism such a potential problem, it seems that we had better improve our quality control of food to discover and prevent contamination from that source before it is too late. It might be easier than we imagine for a terrorist group to cause chaos in this way. Unfortunately, that and many other gaps in our security programs are not being addressed, perhaps because of our huge indebtedness and governmental lethargy.

Occasionally, even foodstuffs grown or raised here in the United States are found to be defective – again, usually after many people have suffered illness. The practicality of eliminating such problems to any level nearing perfection is virtually not possible, but there should be an achievable level that would minimize the probability of such a problem resulting from terrorism.

The Influence of Business

20. Business Affects Social Harmony

The prevalence and nature of change in the world of business have become almost as varied as the weather. Most management books in recent years have cited examples of fine managers in excellent companies with accent on their admirable skills. Many of them, both managers and companies, have suffered severe reverses within the past few years. The managers remained dynamic and excellent in their management styles only by old definitions that are no longer valid. The worldwide marketplace has provided chaotic conditions of change in which the need for aggressive responses has come from unpredictable sources – some that defeat planning. The recent need for complete reorganization of IBM and the former survival problems of Apple Computer, one of the most innovative companies ever in the field of computers, are examples. Major airlines and international banking institutions also provide examples of large "model" business organizations that have had to fight for survival. Being a corporate CEO today almost requires a "black belt" in the art of coping with and beating the vicissitudes of the market.

The influence of business on areas of social harmony that society either lacks or enjoys is much greater than generally is realized. If, for example, we consider a "company town" in which the company employs five thousand people locally and the entire town population is fifty thousand, a good company management style will have a profound effect on the population. Bartlesville, Oklahoma, the home of Phillips Petroleum (since merged with Conoco Oil) is such a town. With five thousand employees leaving work each night happier for having spent the workday in a pleasant environment, the town should enjoy:

- Happier families with less divorce
- Less crime
- Children achieving better in school
- Reduced incidence of mental illness
- The need for fewer police and a higher quality of life, with less divisiveness between political parties, ethnic groups, or social strata

With such positive influence on the social well-being of the company town, it is easy to see how important good management, integrated throughout the business world, can be for society. If only business managers realized the extent of their social importance! The expression "trickle-down", which so often is applied to economics, would really apply to the benefits that could accrue to both business and society were business leaders to attach appropriate significance to having happy employees. Many of the social ills that tend to push us toward chaos would be reduced appreciably. Our quality of life could be improved immensely as a result of enhanced social harmony. This type of thinking requires a long-range attitude. The benefits would not happen overnight. But even the long-term economic benefits to businesses could be surprisingly strong.

Because such a strong beneficial impact on society indirectly results from good management culture, in which good interpersonal relationships and team attitudes are stressed, business schools should be persuaded to inculcate their students with this precept. Business leaders also must learn that, like entertainers, they are often in the public eye and always on view to their associates. In such roles they influence public morale inordinately. It becomes disconcerting to observers when business leaders become so self-serving and obnoxiously greedy as to think they deserve monetary reward that infinitely exceeds what might be considered justified. Were you to add the salary plus typical "perks" and divide it by 2600 (fifty hours per week times fifty-two weeks per year), you would find that a large number of these leaders are paid well over $10,000 per hour. And that does not include the huge retirement benefits they have built into their employment package, usually without stockholder approval. Then, on top of all that, to include in their employment package a multi-million-dollar "golden parachute" in case their publicly owned company is bought out, is greed at its worst. That they may be deprived of a job in the event of such a buyout can easily be taken care of by providing an employment contract. Perhaps the worst example of such greed is that of a former CEO of the New York Stock Exchange who retired with a golden package of a few hundred million dollars, a provision so well written into his employment package that it defied legal challenge.

In a May 2009 article in Forbes Magazine on the subject of *Executive Pay*, Emily Lambert makes several provocative statements. Her research concludes that chief executive pay grew from 40 times average workers pay in 1980 to 433 times in 2007. Talk about greed and complicit automatic sanction of excessive pay by friendly board members! Ms. Lambert also refers to company payment of personal financial planning, personal use of company aircraft, providing of home security, and payment of taxes on perks, all of which can add to a considerable sum that often is not evident in data provided to stockholders. She refers to a "Lake Wobegon effect: everyone struggling to be paid above average".

When the Ten Commandments were written, they probably addressed the ten most common types of sin at the time. Were they to be rewritten today, an eleventh type of sin would certainly have to be added: "Thou shalt not exhibit greed".

On live television, Wednesday, February 11, 2009 a group of large banking institution CEOs were defending their use of government bailout funds. At least two indicated that their organizations were only involved in banking services for other banking firms. They all expressed understanding of the public's displeasure with their industry. Two of them made a statement to the effect that they did not use government funds for bonuses or other purposes that were subject to disapproval. Those utterances completely overlooked the thought that had large bonuses and other acts of extravagance not occurred those monies could have been applied to reduce the need for government funds.

Warren Buffett, chairman of Berkshire Hathaway Corp., is living proof that it is not necessary to evidence greed to become successful. His business achievements are legendary, and not merely because he oversees a huge business empire. He does so with a minimum of typical corporate hierarchy because of the trust and faith he conveys to those reporting to him. His lifestyle is exemplary, without any display of extravagance, and he communicates well with his employees and stockholders. Several years ago a friend of mine who has been a stockholder in Berkshire Hathaway for a long time showed me a communication from the company asking which charity he wanted the company to donate to, in his name, as part of their year-end policy. They wanted their charity contributions, in proportion to each stockholder's share of corporate ownership, to be given to a charity of the stockholder's choice. What a contrast to the more typical self-serving CEO!

21. Time Marches Backwards

It is certainly annoying to place an impersonal business telephone call and have to go through a litany of instructions telling you to press certain buttons in response to a series of questions. This is a time-consuming ordeal that you could have covered with a live person in one-fourth of the time. And, before those instructions are given, you are often asked whether you can speak in English or need to speak in Spanish – a question usually posed to give the braggadocio impression that you that you are speaking to a "big-time" outfit. Then, after you believe you are finally going to get to talk to a non-robotic communicator, you are hit with the question: What are the last four digits of your Social Security number? If, as is usually my problem, you do not have your Social Security number committed to memory, you then have to hang up, look it up, and then start all over. Twenty years ago, things were simpler. Perhaps a business saves money with these new, annoying communication approaches, but is not the customer's time also of some value?

Have you recently had occasion to call a manufacturer for technical support relative to an appliance or computer-related device and found you were talking to somebody from India? This is so common because outsourcing the technical support department to India takes advantage of the lower wage rates prevalent in India, producing sufficient savings to more than offset the added costs of outsourcing. Totally neglected is the fact that, even with much training, such Indian personnel have accents difficult to understand – especially for the hard of hearing. This is not a reflection on intelligence or training. These are problems that can and very frequently do result in frustrating and unsatisfactory communication. Tom Friedman in his book *The World is Flat* refers to this communication problem.

I recently agreed, while seeking technical support, and having to talk with someone in Mumbai, to purchase a new printer after being assured that it would be compatible with the computer software I was using. That decision followed assurance that the new printer would cost so little more than repairing my old one as to make such repairs not worthwhile.

The new printer arrived and was not compatible with the software I had been using. I was forced to call India again. It was another long and annoying hassle, and I was unable to find a way to contact the American manufacturer in the United States. Finally resolving my problem proved to be more annoying an experience than I ever intend to expose myself to again.

Everyone with whom I have discussed this problem has agreed they would rather pay a manufacturer a considerably higher price and be able to talk to a technician who actually works domestically for them.

These problems, offshoots of our new information technology age, were not existent a generation ago. They serve to make life less pleasant today, which is why the title of this topic is "Time Marches Backwards". They are true examples of suppliers being totally inconsiderate of the customer. When we customers finally revolt, in some fashion, suppliers will be forced to take a different approach – at least, one hopes so!

Section VI

Government Controls

Introduction

Governmental regulations are so numerous as to almost defy sufficient familiarity to permit conformance in the case of many industries. The serious need for regulatory reform has been discussed and re-discussed so many times in Congress, without any resulting action, that the public and the business community in particular, are disgusted. The subject has become the object of much humor. A recent cartoon in *The Wall Street Journal* depicts two dogs in a dog pound cage. One says to the other, "The E.P.A. nailed me for digging up my own bones".

Groucho Marx once said, "Politics is the art of looking for trouble, finding it, misdiagnosing it and then misapplying the wrong remedies". Certainly, most of our politicians are well-meaning and intelligent; nonetheless, Groucho's statement is true too often.

22. Occupational Safety and Health

The government agency having to do with occupational health and safety is the known as OSHA. In many cases it has unnecessarily burdened industry, but it has also made industry much more safety and health conscious. Overall, it is certainly having a positive impact.

The continuing problem with OSHA is that they often issue an edict requiring that businesses make changes without allowing sufficient participation by business in making such rulings. OSHA's regulations can cause excessive costs to achieve the desired result. An example of this is a requirement issued in the mid-1990s that the elevator access buttons in all buildings be low enough to provide easy access to wheelchair users. Certainly, the concept was meritorious, but the arbitrary positioning required an exact location so many inches from floor level. The elevator access buttons in many buildings were already easily reachable by people in wheelchairs, but building owners had to move them at great expense to conform to OSHA's arbitrary location. If you worked in such a building, as I did, you would have observed that walls had to be broken into, electrical connections and wiring had to be moved, and elevator service was inconvenient during the long time required to make these changes. Further, after completion of the electrical and building revisions, the redecorating cost was appreciable. The total cost was sufficient to require in a rent increase in some cases.

The same problem was often the case with the requirement that all guard railings had to be so many inches above the floor line. The intent was good, but much unnecessary expense was incurred because they did not have the foresight to provide reasonable variance in the case of existing guard railings. Again, much unnecessary cost to industry resulted. OSHA needs to plan better and seek greater participation from business in their well-intentioned work.

23. Income Taxes

Certainly, a system of taxation is necessary for our government to function; and, to the degree that it is structured so as to be fair to all, we should respectfully comply with our tax laws. If all taxation – federal, state, and local – combines in such a manner as to be disproportionately burdensome to any segment of society, ultimately chaos will occur. Then, even those who thought they were blessed by being members of a portion of society that enjoyed less than average taxation, will wish they had paid their fair share. Of course, "fair share" is difficult to define. If at least two nonpartisan "think tank" groups were to brainstorm the subject and reach consensus, it is likely that a reasonable "fair share" definition could be reached.

That scenario would surely provide for indexing with inflation and take into consideration a minimum lifestyle income level, often referred to as "poverty level". (The expression "poverty level" is truly demeaning for those to whom it might apply and should be replaced.) It should also reflect consideration for the number of dependents in the family.

Once "fair share" is defined, total tax goals and methods of taxation could be determined. Again, nonpartisan and nonpolitical "think tank" groups should be used to propose the final tax code. Certainly, members of Congress should participate in this process to provide pragmatism and participative communication. After all, the conclusions will require "selling" to all branches of government and to the public at large. With our tax code now exceeding 67,000 pages, the need for simplification is long overdue.

In 1995, an article from Cox News Service cited that a study by the United States Census Bureau indicated that the poorest 20 percent of non-elderly married couples paid 12.5 percent of their income in state and local taxes, the richest 1 percent paid just 7.9 percent, and the middle 60 percent paid 9.8 percent. Changes made during the George W. Bush administration have made the percentage advantage of the rich over the poor even greater. The 1995 study was conducted at the behest of what may be described as a liberal-leaning policy research group but is represented as being actuarially accurate.

Such a situation is caused largely by overdependence on sales taxes for state and city revenue. Sales taxes have no regard for a person's economic status. In some states sales tax is applied to food and drugs, and in other states sales tax is not applied to food and drugs. That may or may not be justified, but it is usually decided by politicians without impartial, enlightened discussion. Given a proper decision-making scenario, we might prevent the condition in some states in which the poor pay as much as four times the proportion of their income as the rich. In states where they rely on graduated income taxes and have relatively low or no sales tax, such large disparity does not occur. The same study indicated that there was little relationship between a state's taxation system and its economic health and rate of growth.

A seldom-realized pyramiding flaw in our taxation system is that as wages are increased some percentage to offset inflation, merely to permit the taxpayer to have equal spending power, that increase in wages can put the employee into a higher tax rate bracket. This can and often does result in net income being less than before, insofar as spending power is concerned.

A report released by the United States Census Bureau in June 1996, and reported in *The Wall Street Journal*, indicates that the United States is becoming more economically polarized than at any time since World War II. This probably means we are more economically polarized than at any point in our history. Poor and middle-class families were getting a growing share of the nation's wealth until the mid-1960's, but since then that trend has reversed. The share of our nation's economic pie enjoyed by the richest one-fifth of American families had increased from 40.9 percent in 1970 to 46.9 percent in 1994. The top 5 percent of families increased their share from 15.6 percent to 20.1 percent of the pie. There are many reasons given for this trend. Among them are the stagnation of wage levels for low-skilled workers, the increasing reliance on "high-tech" vocations, and the huge increases in earnings for those with special talents, particularly in the areas of entertainment and sports. The trend to two-income families also has had considerable impact. Exponential increases in earnings for corporate CEO's are also very evident. When salaries, bonuses, stock options, retirement wages, and other fringe benefits often add up to well over $10,000 per hour, how can people at the lower economic levels be expected to understand? It is a given that no person's talents are irreplaceable. Therefore, how can any person be worth over $10,000 per hour?

Regardless of the reasons, if this trend continues, at some future time it can be the cause of severe social problems. It is mentioned here since one of the major influences we have for slowing down the concentration of wealth, which produces economic polarization, is through our taxation policies. Certainly, education and job training can also help individually, but they do not create jobs. Only increased demand for goods and services results in more jobs.

In a Wall Street Journal article dated July 23, 2008 Jesse Drucker reported that IRS data from the year 2006 indicates the richest 1 percent of Americans enjoyed the highest adjusted gross income for the past two decades. The same year, figures also indicate that the wealthiest 1 percent enjoyed the lowest tax rate in over eighteen years, indicating that their income share was growing.

Several years ago, former Senator Mike Synar pointed out to me that according to an IRS analysis, the amount of undeclared income tax liability was very large–perhaps as much as seventy billion dollars per year. Today that sum is no doubt much higher. I asked his opinion as to whether the requirement of proof of having filed the previous year's income tax liability forms with the IRS when applying for credit or employment would help ferret out these tax evaders. If the IRS discovered you had been a tax evader as a result of not having filed yearly reports, their subsequent claims against you could certainly have an adverse effect on your creditworthiness. Therefore, though it might be considered regimentation, and might require additional paperwork by the IRS and the business community at large, the huge amount of money involved would easily justify such an approach.

In discussing the matter further, we realized that many details would have to be worked out so that the implementation of such a program would not be unfair in some instances, such as the first time someone applies for a job. He asked me to write him a letter on the subject for his further study; but, as I was not in his congressional district and was, at that time, pressured for time, I failed to do so.

In addition to the failure on the part of many people to fully pay their income taxes an article in U.S.A. Today dated October 31, 2008 cites a report from the Internal Revenue Service in which the amount of fraudulent tax refunds exceed $1.6 billion dollars, a huge sum being drained from our government by citizens who can be compared to common thieves.

Perhaps the issuance of some form of paper work to those citizens who have not properly declared their income tax liability, or the absence of liability, could perform another function. It could be required for consideration in one's application for admission to the military or before being registered to vote. Of course, there are many possible exceptions that might have to be considered, but much false representation could be prevented or made evident. Could it also have a positive effect on the quality of voters?

The inefficiency and excessive size of our government has resulted in "Tax Freedom Day" occurring fifty-nine days later in 1995 than it did in 1940, according to the Tax Foundation. "Tax Freedom Day" is the date at which the average person would have paid all of his or her tax obligations for the year if all of their income up to that time were used for that purpose. Although over one-third of those fifty-nine days was due to the Second World War, it is a disturbing thought that typically, we must work from the first of the year until May sixth to pay our taxes, as was the case in 1995. Now, over a decade later, "Tax Freedom Day" is probably closer to June first.

At the time of this writing, there is much discussion of a flat tax to replace the very complex graduated tax structure the United States now has. In the debate over the fairness or un-fairness of a flat tax, those who would benefit most, to the dismay of all liberals, would be those with the highest incomes. The poor, who now pay no income tax, would be free of tax until their income exceeded $40 thousand for a married couple, for example. The middle class would or would not notice much difference, depending on who is doing the evaluating.

In January 1996, the well-known columnist Thomas Sowell made the following startling observation: "The reason the country can gain from changing to a flat tax is that the cost to a taxpayer for preparing his tax return, including accountants and their secretaries and offices, often exceeds his or her tax liability". If this statement is even close to being valid, there is a dire need to revise our tax code. It is close to producing chaos. Because his observation in 1996 might not be as germane today, I exchanged e-mails with Dr. Sowell in February 2009 and in his response, he stated "It is a case of what economists call 'dead weight losses' where the recipient receives less than the total cost to those from which the money came – that is, including both the actual payment itself and the costs associated with making that payment". With a flat tax, of course, those costs would be largely reduced and additional income to the government would result from taxes paid on the resulting savings. The government would also save from the large reduction in Internal Revenue Service personnel, the probably reduction in fraudulent tax returns and fraudulent claims for tax refunds.

No one seems to be considering a type of graduated flat tax, which might be graduated from a lowest level of perhaps 15 percent to a highest level of perhaps 28 percent, the graduations based on income. Considerations such as charity contributions or home mortgages would have to be debated as part of any tax code revision. A graduated flat tax might meet the objections of those concerned that the wealthy should pay at a much higher level than the middle class. It would reduce the cost of collecting taxes and would appreciably increase voluntary compliance by the public. The huge reduction in the cost of tax collecting and record keeping would permit tax reduction for all. The lower level of taxation would make such a tax program palatable for all, even those who previously were "gung-ho" on eliminating the taxation of dividends and capital gains or indexing capital gains to compensate for inflation. Even though graduated, such a revision of our tax code could still be thought of as being "flat" in that it would still be a fixed percentage without most of the special deductions now allowed and could be reported using but a one or two page return form.

The *National Taxpayers Union and the National Taxpayers Union Foundation*, in September of 2005, issued their *NTUF Policy Paper 15* which noted that many foreign countries have adopted a flat tax and are happy with it. They also noted that over 6.6 billion hours are spent by Americans in preparing their tax returns.

It might be well to put this topic of taxes in better perspective by considering the purpose of taxation in a democracy: first, providing funds for the operation of and defense of the nation and secondly, to insure that democracy continues "ad infinitum" rather than permitting the spread between the rich and the poor to become so pronounced as to become more like survival of the strongest. With our federal deficit being in "the stratosphere", reforming our tax code represents an area for huge savings.

24. So What?

That we have still enjoyed relatively low unemployment compared to many other nations seems to justify the attitude "if it ain't broke, don't fix it" on the part of government. That was the case before the financial reversal we suffered in late 2008. With that financial reversal came the realization that much of the cause could have been a failure of government to sufficiently control banking institutions and minimize the prevalence of greed in publicly owned businesses.

The continuing trend of an increasing percentage of our "economic pie" being enjoyed by the wealthy and a decreasing percentage by the middle and lower classes is approaching a critical stage and truly must be addressed. Yes, there are attempts to ameliorate this trend with changes in Medicare and possibly in Social Security, but such efforts, although also necessary, will but postpone the arrival of severe social unrest. There is even the long-range possibility that such unrest can border on, if not be a cause for, insurrection.

The manner in which government funds extended in late 2008 to many organizations in financial distress were handled indicates a warped perspective on the part of many, if not most, corporate executives as to how much remuneration they are worth. That they could rationalize the taking of huge bonuses in 2008 after suffering bad losses was viewed as unconscionable by the public. This was discussed in Topic 23 "Income Taxes" but no corrective action was suggested. So far, attempts to use taxation as a means of limiting salaries, bonuses, and other expensive amenities given to CEOs of publicly held corporations have proven to be ineffective. There are too many possible loopholes to be found. What has not been tried is making remuneration above some reasonable amount, such as one million dollars, unlawful without stockholder approval. The reaction of CEOs to such a proposal would probably include "How can people who are not in our "financial shoes" and who do not face important decision-making as we must every day have perspective to fairly decide what we are worth?" The obvious disclaimer to that contention is that if the stockholders were allowed one vote per share of stock, the majority of votes would be by stockholders owning larger numbers of shares who, for the most part, are sufficiently "well-off" to be able to apply rational perspective to such an issue. Many stockholders I know of, me included, faced with the voting we are permitted before stockholders meetings, arbitrarily vote no on issues such as retirement funding as a way to limit exorbitant remuneration but these few votes are limited in power. Were other remuneration factors reasonable, I would certainly approve modest retirement funding.

Section VII

The Process of Government

25. Our Withering Democracy

We in the United States feel that everyone should live in a democratic society. This assumption is proven wrong every time we try to impose democracy in any other country. As we are finding out, ever so slowly, people who have been living under any other type of government find it difficult to adapt to democracy all of sudden. They might find it a more welcome change were it imposed gradually, so they do not lose their sense of security.

The spirit of democracy in the United States no longer prevails as intended by our Founding Fathers. The process by which, as citizens, we influence or change the direction of our government has become too difficult. In fact, most of us often find that the best we can do is to vote against a candidate; rarely do we enjoy the privilege of voting for a candidate. The occasional questionnaires we receive from our representatives in Congress are so inane as to be mere promotional exercises. The answers to such questions as, "Do you believe we should decrease foreign aid?" absolutely have no meaningful use. The question is much too complex to be answered by a "yes" or "no", and those constituents to whom such questions are directed rarely have sufficient knowledge upon which to base an answer. The answers received are used for propaganda purposes at best. Members of Congress who issue such questionnaires may not realize it, but in doing so they are pandering to the public.

The majority of people elected to government positions have no managerial experience nor do they participate in the type of debate process that produces decisions which stand the test of time. Worse yet, although many of them are what we think of as "good people", they receive inadequate training after reaching office to perform properly in what proves to be a completely new environment for them. For the most part, they operate on instinct, with the strongest influence being "what will gain me reelection". They are pressured to go along with the aims of the party regardless of their personal opinions. They quickly learn that being in government does not require efficient use of the people's money. In the worst case, they soon acquire a sense of greed that provides them a lifetime of security plus tax-free "perks" that would not be allowed to the average citizen by the Internal Revenue Service.

Such conditions in our government must change or they will cause our undoing. They are capable of producing chaos! Yes, we can brag that we have the best country in the world, and certainly the United States has enjoyed the longest and best democratic experience the world has seen, but current trends are not good. In September 1995, while being interviewed about the criminal behavior of some of his first-string players, the football coach of the University of Nebraska commented on the character typical of his recruits today compared to those of thirty years earlier. He pointed out that the prevalence of dysfunctional families has resulted in a serious decline in behavior patterns of his available recruits. The situation he observed is a common problem for sport coaches, but many of these recruits, under the paternalistic influence of their coaches, do manage to achieve well for four years and move on to "mega-salaries" in professional sports. The "mega-salaries" and dysfunctional families are both reflections of the decline of civility in our society and the tremendous increase in the number of sociopaths among us. That so many of them fail to graduate school is another problem. The "mega-salaries" have made professional sports so expensive that many people, me included, will not attend professional sporting events. Today, a family of four must budget almost $400 to attend a baseball game, for example, when you include the cost of tickets, car expense, and refreshments.

Dr. Richard Caroming, United States Surgeon General from 2002 to 2006, told Congress, according to *Wall Street Journal* reporter Laura Meckler, that he was continually thwarted by the Bush administration from speaking his mind on important medically-oriented subjects. He was, he said, also told to include reference to President Bush at least three times per page in each of his speeches. In addition, his speeches had to be submitted to administration appointees for approval and virtual rewriting. He says he was blocked at every turn. For the executive branch of government to exert controlling influence on government-at-large to such an extent is reprehensible and certainly contrary to the basics of democracy.

Our voting process is particularly flawed in that too often people knowingly or inadvertently vote in response to the influence of self-motivated organizations such as the gun lobby or the highly organized Christian Coalition of America. Influenced by either of these organizations, voters rarely vote as a result of their own thinking. For example, how can a thinking person feel that the average citizen has potential need for terrorist-like automatic weapons capable of firing multiple rounds of ammunition per second? At election time, however, the large expenditures of money by the gun lobby causes a "red-necked" majority to avidly vote almost as a solid bloc while the rest of the voting public takes its usual nonchalant attitude, showing up at the polls only if it is convenient.

In 1994, there was a marked tendency among voters to reject the "ins" and elect new members to Congress. Perhaps this was a factor in the large swing from a Democrat majority to a Republican majority. Events of the following year suggest that the voters' revolt did not effect much change. Professor Robert Fogel of the University of Chicago refers, in a January 1996 *Wall Street Journal* article, to exit polls taken in 1982. Those polls revealed that about one-third of voters identified themselves as evangelicals. He refers to them as "believers in enthusiastic religions" and says that in 1994, approximately one-fourth of that group voted Democratic and three-fourths voted Republican. He concludes that such statistics reveal that we are in a process of political change largely spawned by trends in American religiosity.

We all know that our country's Founding Fathers endeavored to keep politics free of religion in consideration of our religious diversity, and virtually all social scientists agree that their decision was and still is loaded with wisdom. It is very unlikely that any religious group's attitude formation process can be objective. By and large, such a group attitude derives from – or, in effect, is imposed by – a preaching exposure. Contrary thought is often considered heretic. This increasing and highly organized power of our "enthusiastic religions" has caused a 25 percent reduction in membership in Protestant mainline churches and a near doubling of membership in the "enthusiastic" churches. Professor Fogel refers to this trend as "The Fourth Great Awakening", and states that each awakening has brought about long-lasting change. Without some unexpected reversal, this process of political change may have a cycle of many decades with a negative long-term effect on our politics.

Senator Mike Synar died of cancer in January 1996. Politicians of both parties and editors from all over the country paid tribute to him. *The Chicago Sun-Times* referred to him in their January 10th, 1966 edition as a "brave and unflinching public servant who, in tough political times, remained true to his principles". He was considered an example of the ideal congressman. Nevertheless, when he ran for reelection in 1994, the National Rifle Association gave huge sums of money to defeat him. This was revenge for his adamant campaign against the sale of automatic weapons to the public and for the requirement of a seven-day wait before being granted a gun license. He was defeated in the primary by a politically unknown retired school teacher who did little campaigning and lost to the rival Republican – as planned by the NRA. This is an example of the sad state of our election process when an organization such as the National Rifle Association can wield so much influence as to replace a highly respected candidate with an unknown and plan for the unknown to go "by the boards".

In my previous book *Stealth Management: With Shared Goals, They Will Hardly Know You Are Leading Them,* reference is made to a typical university mission statement which would include the aim to educate students in a way that makes them more apt to be happy and therefore potentially better parents. With the assertion "We can assume that if all people were brought up well, and in happy families, the world would have fewer problems", the book then goes on to say, "It therefore would seem appropriate for the university to offer a course in parenting and social responsibility". Certainly, teaching good parenting and social responsibility to all students at the high school and college levels would be an important factor in addressing the causes of social "mal de mer". Back in the period between 1930 and 1945 most of our better high schools had a course in Civics, usually required of seniors. In the Civics course to which I was exposed in New Jersey, the teacher had all students receive the *New York Herald Tribune*, then a highly respected newspaper. The day following receipt of the newspaper, we discussed one or more of the editorials. Our teacher never evidenced social bias or gave opinions. Instead, he provoked discussion and, when necessary, led us through the discussion technique of asking questions. It was largely like the "Great Books" discussions. The editorials we discussed usually helped us develop a better personal value system in addition to alerting us to the need for social responsibility. At that time, there was no parental obstructionism based on religious concerns. Today such an uplifting influence on our young people would not be permitted by the evangelical religious right – a very negative change for our society.

Today, in the interest of keeping the cost of education as low as possible, most school districts have eliminated many adjunct courses such as Art, Music, and Civics. The need for busing to provide equal and integrated education requires so many students to leave the school environs immediately after classes that many social activities such as language clubs, glee club, chess club, nature club, orchestra, science club, and the like have all but disappeared. Such non-credit courses were of tremendous social benefit and used much of the student's spare time more constructively than do gangs and carousing. If the long-term value of such school programs were compared to the increased cost of crime and school dropout programs, voters would have solid reason to ensure that they returned to the school campus, even if taxes went up in the short term. The recognized need for these programs might motivate voters to find a better answer than busing to integrate the schools. Thinking along these lines addresses the causes of social problems more effectively than building prisons.

Our process of government does need change, and we must address the causes of social unrest, not merely their symptoms, more emphatically. It is quite easy to show that these causes are also large contributors to many of our problems, including the huge budget deficit. We are blessed to live in a country where politics do exist, for in those countries where politics, in the conventional sense, do not exist, there is lack of freedom and little need to ever vote. Michael Black, formerly a business executive and dean of St. Benet's Hall, Oxford, says, "Politics in the classical sense is about ways of doing things collectively given that people think differently. Classical politics recognizes that if we don't control our own behavior in response to the behavior of others, we can do very little together – regardless of the way we think". In the United States, the danger-ous desire of organized groups to impose their thinking, without regard for others, does not fit within that classi-cal definition of politics. It destroys politics. In fact, such group action if not contained within some reasonable bounds, can endanger the continuation of democracy as we know it.

In his syndicated column of May 14, 1997, in the Wash-ington Post, David Broder, referring to a proposed bal-anced budget agreement, called it "a minimalist agree-ment, a lowest-common-denominator compromise". He then added, "There was no reason to expect anything more from a government as politically weak as ours. In-deed, if the politicians running our government had made any decision that actually made a significant difference, they would be acting unlike themselves". Broder's opin-ion, unfortunately, is shared by a large percentage of our thinking citizens.

In addition to the situation described in the foregoing commentary on our withering democracy, we are nega-tively impacted by many of our political and religious lead-ers, who exhibit extreme levels of greed, self-righteous-ness, intransigence and piety. Of course, extreme piety is harmful only insofar as it intrudes on government and education in a manner that the architects of our Constitu-tion tried to prevent.

If you are inclined to lump all the foregoing problems in a batch with the hope that "even though things may have to get worse before they get better, all will be well in the end", please consider the demise of the Roman Empire. The Roman Empire was the most dominant nation on earth in its time, and perhaps its dominance has never been equaled. It excelled in virtually all areas of influence – military, industrial, farming, art, education, etc. It also, like the United States, suffered from excesses such as greed, over consumption, and diminished participation in government by the people. Its demise occurred over a relatively short period, historically speaking. Could we be headed the same way? Statistics indicate that we are already falling behind in many areas: medically, in terms of infant mortality; educationally; and in global influence, as indicated by the low esteem in which we are held internationally.

CNN, in a recent documentary-like presentation, reviewed and interviewed a group of Americans living in Paris. They were very content with their life in France and found it much more to their liking than their former lives in the United States, where there was so much crime, political folderol, and greed. They are not the only such group in France, and there are numerous counterparts in Canada, Mexico, United Kingdom and other countries. There are also many people living in the United States who are unhappy with domestic trends and are seriously considering moving to other countries. Most of us and our government seem unaware of these discontents or choose to ignore the significance of the increase in their number. This phenomenon, as described by CNN, is indicative of and further evidence of our withering democracy.

26. Our Federal Budget in Perspective

It is very difficult to put our dire financial condition into reasonable perspective. Perhaps it would help to note that our overall federal budget is approximately $3 trillion for fiscal year 2008. That and the following data are quoted from an article by Jeffrey D. Sachs, an economist and the director of the Earth Institute at Columbia University. Professor Sachs points out that our federal expenditures are divided as follows:

- 25 percent - Social Security, including disability – $750 Billion
- 24 percent - Medicare, veterans' benefits – $720 Billion
- 20 percent - Defense – $600 Billion
- 8 percent - Interest on public debt – $240 Billion
- 23 percent - all other government expenses, which would include energy, commerce, agriculture, community development, science, international affairs, environment, government operations, transportation, education, and at least four other categories lumped under the description "income security" – $690 Billion

All of the categories above are subject to variation from year to year. Professor Sachs predicted that during 2008, the United States would experience a budget deficit of approximately $500 billion and perhaps much higher because of the $750 billion financial bailout. It has been estimated by Chairman Bernanke that since the bailout will largely be represented by the purchase of financial institutional bonds, most of it will be repaid, albeit very slowly. If we assume that in a worst-case scenario our deficit could reach $600 billion in 2008, it would then be higher than ever in history.

Obviously, to reverse the trend of increasing debt requires that the total of the five categories of federal expenditures must each be reduced over 20 percent for us to merely break even. Reducing our indebtedness significantly over time would probably require a reduction of between 25 percent and 30 percent. A 25 percent reduction would require us to eliminate $750 billion of expenses (25 percent of $3 trillion). A 30 percent reduction would require us to somehow eliminate $900 billion of expenses (30 percent of $3 trillion). All these reduction figures would only be effective after interest on our indebtedness has been paid.

The gross interest paid on public debt cannot be reduced except by reducing debt itself. Defense is a category that can be greatly reduced after we terminate our war in Iraq. Further savings are possible by eliminating our military presence in Europe and gradually doing so in Korea. Let's assume that we could, over three years, reduce our defense budget from 20 percent to 8 percent. That would amount to a savings of $360 billion (12 percent of $900 billion) and still require additional reductions from the other three categories totaling between $390 billion and $540 billion. Such reductions seem almost impossible.

27. Is The United States Broke Financially?

If we were to audit our government's financial condition in a manner similar to a CPA's audit of a business, we would probably be told that we are irretrievably bankrupt and beyond the potential salvation usually provided by Chapter 11 bankruptcy. A business that finds itself unable to meet its financial obligations usually has to file for bankruptcy. If it can present to the court a plan that provides for a reasonable possibility of reorganization and subsequent discharge of debts, the court will provide time for that to occur and those to whom money is owed are put on hold during that interval. That is referred to as Chapter 11 bankruptcy. If there is not evidence that such a successful reorganization is likely, the court decrees the business to have failed, in which case its assets must be sold and the monies generated, after expenses (including very large legal expenses) equitably dispersed among the creditors. After this process referred to as Chapter 7 bankruptcy, the business no longer exists.

During the Clinton administration our government ostensibly enjoyed a decrease in its level of indebtedness. The adverb "ostensibly" is applicable because had "off-balance-sheet" items been included, our indebtedness would have been seen to rise even during the Clinton administration.

Our government often is guilty, sad to say, of using the numbers to tell the desired story rather than to present the truth. We are given numbers relating to inflation that represent what is called "core inflation", which excludes several items such as the cost of fuel. That is why, during 2007 and 2008, we are told that inflation is of little consequence, while our real cost of living is rising rapidly and many families are having severe financial difficulty. Another example of such deception has to do with our payments into the Social Security fund, a fund that exists to provide for retirement and several types of disability benefits. That fund will soon suffer from insufficient income to exercise its obligations in spite of the several changes made by Congress to alleviate the problem. In fact, it is not income to the government for ongoing operations. When the government uses these monies for other purposes, it is really borrowing from the Social Security fund. That it pays token (not competitive) interest for the use of those funds is certainly evidence that such borrowing represents indebtedness rather than income. Instead, it represents these "off-balance-sheet" items as federal income which, in concept, is intended to make things less worrisome to the public and give us less reason to be critical of our government's performance.

Our severe imbalance of trade further exacerbates our financial well-being and is a major influence in the decline of the dollar. Many countries fight such negative influences by exacting import duties. Such actions, in turn, can result in the use of duties revengefully applied on the goods we export. Such trade controls are seldom of long-term benefit, although unfair trade practices by foreign manufacturers sometimes do justify them.

Meanwhile, our total federal indebtedness has reached the preposterous level of almost $10 trillion and would be over that by year end 2008 according to Andrew Yarrow's book *Everlasting Debt*. He also refers to the promise by our government to pay another $50 trillion or so in explicit benefits in the future. Although that future obligation is probably due to Social Security and Medicare, Mr. Yarrow did not specify this. Dividing such indebtedness by the number of families paying significant taxes equates to almost a million dollars per family. After all, whatever hope we have for paying that indebtedness will have to be borne by the taxpayers, mostly by those from families that are the more significant taxpayers. It is a level of indebtedness that now seems beyond reasonable methods for solution. The obvious solutions are either increased taxes or a decrease in expenses. The fact that many other countries have severe indebtedness, measured as a percentage of their gross national product even greater that ours should not justify any attempt to rationalize this potentially chaotic problem. In January of 1992, Argentina, faced with the same problem, finally changed its currency, making the previously used currency almost worthless. Imagine the implications of such action in the United States. As stated before, if our country was viewed as a business, we could not qualify for Chapter 11 bankruptcy but would be forced into Chapter 7 bankruptcy.

At the time of the election, none of the leading presidential candidates of 2008 evidenced understanding of these dire financial conditions, which are continuing to worsen. According to Andrew Taylor, of the *Associated Press*, the White House predicted that our 2009 federal deficit would reach $482 billion, and that does not include the many billions in additional funding needed for our wars in Iraq and Afghanistan. Further, with the stock market (as of July, 2008) in virtual bear market territory, the White House assumptions are probably (as usual, regardless of which party is in power) overly optimistic.

In September of 2008, we experienced a near meltdown of Wall Street and many of its financial institutions, an event so serious as to be felt around the world. Government intervention, which has met with questioning approval, may "save the day", but salvaging organizations which are guilty of both greed and mismanagement while others do not get such undeserved treatment seems very unfair to many. It does not permit the normal forces of business to punish or reward properly; it also contributes to inflation. Unfortunately, as indicated by Federal Reserve Chairman Bernanke, the need for government intervention is so severe that withholding it could cause severe individual suffering; thus, it is the best available option in spite of its many shortcomings.

I certainly do not wish to be a purveyor of gloom, as all the foregoing commentary might imply. There are many possible steps we can take to solve our long-term problems, but only if we act effectively and soon. Unfortunately, because such steps may require a marked adjustment in our lifestyles and mores, changes that our society might find repugnant, necessary political action is most unlikely. It would require a high level of understanding and patriotism to inculcate us with sufficient willingness to cooperate.

Some of these possible changes might include the following:

1. As mentioned in Topic 8, our Justice Department estimates that crime costs us over $450 billion per year. Reducing that expense could contribute significantly to alleviating our financial stress.

2. In Topic 23, former senator Mike Synar is quoted as having said, "An IRS study indicated that under-declared tax liability in our country exceeded $70 billion per year and is vastly higher now". Perhaps an honor system such as used in some colleges should be used with regard to our under-declared taxes. Certainly many of us know of people who are guilty of such malfeasance. Yes, squealing on such people seems abhorrent, but if it is a necessary change to help prevent the United States from literally going bankrupt, would it not become an acceptable, even patriotic, practice? Besides, it would soon virtually eliminate cheating on one's taxes. Of course, before activating such an honor system there ought to be a three to six months period of amnesty giving people the opportunity to voluntarily pay up without penalty. A recent article from the Associated Press also refers to fraudulent tax refunds now exceeding $1 billion. Revising our tax system might also serve to reduce under-declared taxes even without adopting an honor system.

3. Military expenses since 9/11 have already cost us a few trillion dollars. Our dire financial condition justifies refraining from war unless we, or our allies are

attacked. Certainly, preventing the Vietnam and Iraq wars would have saved trillions. The Constitution presumably prevents such capricious military actions, but we apparently find ways to circumvent that limitation.

4. Seriously implementing the energy-saving methods recommended by the Rocky Mountain Institute (see Topic 14) would greatly reduce our consumption of energy, reduce our dependency on foreign oil, reduce our cost of living, and reduce poverty. A tax on excess energy usage, applied by our utility companies, which would apply only to unnecessarily high usage per household, would not only raise federal income but would conserve energy.

5. Decreasing our dependence on foreign oil would lower the cost of the oil we may still need to import and, according to Federal Reserve Chairman Ben Bernanke, it would strengthen the dollar. That, in turn, will help reduce our negative balance of trade. Unfortunately, extreme environmentalists fail to realize the urgency of strengthening the dollar. Certainly, we should care for the environment, but perhaps our dire financial condition merits temporary compromise.

6. Increasing excise taxes, wherever practical, so long as doing so does not have severe negative effects economically or internationally.

7. Increase income taxes on those who are in higher income and/or net worth brackets as recommended by Warren Buffet, who is living proof that high achievement does not require the

greedy attitude so common in our corporate culture.

8. Increase inheritance taxes (also recommended by Warren Buffet).

9. Change Social Security as necessary

10. Reduce the need for government to provide aid to those in need by vastly increasing our voluntary contributions of time and money.

11. Simplify our income taxes. Properly doing so could reduce the vast size of the Internal Revenue Service, the cost of preparation of tax returns, and, probably, the potential for tax cheating of all kinds. Eliminating many types of deductions, such as entertaining expenses, may reduce the cost of recordkeeping and IRS monitoring enough to make many such changes very palatable.

12. With our income tax reporting, provide a line on which we can contribute money, beyond what is owed, toward reducing our national indebtedness. Such contributions should be publicly acknowledged, as is done for those who give to civic organizations such as symphony orchestras, ballet companies, and many charities. A similar provision now permits us to contribute to the cost of presidential political campaigning.

13. In Topic 13, "Soil Depletion and the Hunzas", reference is made to the reason for the saltiness of the oceans: Over the course of eons, salts and minerals are absorbed by rains and then flow into the oceans. From the story therein about the Hunzas we could learn enough to markedly reduce the cost of

Medicare. Ultimately, healthier lifestyles could even permit constructive changes in Social Security.

14. Generally streamline government by eliminating parts that are not cost effective. Given the opportunity to do so, as in the business world-at-large many government employees could and would be forthcoming with cost reducing ideas.

There may be several other sources of savings that a good think tank could arrive at. Solutions for our serious financial problem are available, although very difficult to implement. Worst of all, our leaders seem oblivious of the urgent need to address the problem. If, in addition to replicating the relatively good financial performance during the Clinton administration, we could reduce the cost of government and increase the income to government to provide even a small real reduction of overall United States indebtedness, we would be on the path to recovery. It would not be progress, however, to reduce the cost of federal government by passing it on to the states in a manner that really would not lower the cost to the public.

The continuation of our present financial path to ruin is currently dependent on our on-going ability to sell government bonds as we need to borrow more and more. We largely depend on foreign sources to purchase these debentures. If those foreign sources of credit were to turn us down, we would certainly experience financial chaos. Just as in normal business dealings, a lender will finally balk at extending further credit if the borrower fails to evidence financial responsibility. Indeed, we are playing a very dangerous game by continuing to increase our indebtedness without a plan to pay up which is reflected by our falling dollar. Although the United States dollar has been the primary medium of exchange over most of the world, that is apt to change unless we act to strengthen it.

The continuing decline in the dollar will gradually result in foreign ownership of many of our icon-like assets. Middle Eastern financial interests have purchased the Chrysler building in New York City, for example. The Ford Motor Company sold its Jaguar and Land Rover divisions to a relatively small automobile manufacturer in India and may also have to consider divesting itself of Volvo. The same thing is happening to General Motors. The Trump mansion in Florida was just sold to a foreigner for $100 million. So many of our assets are being purchased by non-Americans, it's scary.

Our military, when evaluating the cost of purchasing from a foreign source, should be made to evaluate the overall cost to our country, not merely the bid price. They should consider that an American company pays United States income taxes, whereas a foreign company does not unless the company has operations in the United States. This was apparently overlooked when they awarded a contract for the manufacture of large flying supertankers used to refuel military aircraft in flight. That contract, fortunately, is being put out for re-bid, although whether the relative United States taxes paid are being considered is unknown.

28. "We the People" as Employers and Managers

Organizations rarely permit employees to vote on their own salaries, benefits, retirement programs, or "perks". In instances when they do, it is usually a part of the organization's culture in which employees, as part of a team effort that is profit-related, appropriately relate remuneration to responsibility, training required, and value produced. In the case of those who hold elective offices, profit is not a consideration, and we have yet to require any qualifications of them other than minimum age, citizenship, and absence of felony conviction. It is the rare politician who has the required perspective to evaluate his or her own value in terms of salary and fringe benefits. In the case of our Congress, their actions in this regard, thus far, have been improperly motivated and entirely self-oriented, and they have resulted in total remuneration, inclusive of fringe benefits, "perks", and retirement benefits, that is grossly excessive. Further, many of their fringe benefits have been implemented in a surreptitious manner, unknown to the voter.

The problem is not just that the cost of government in the United States has become excessive. An even worse result is that the financial cost of our Congress contributes heavily to our prevailing distrust of government. During the partial shutdown of government while the budget was being argued at the end of 1995, a furloughed government employee, who was hurting financially as a result, phoned in to a program being aired on public radio and complained bitterly. She added, "I supervise over 100 employees. If they want to reduce costs in my department, why don't they ask me? I can show them how to cut costs greatly by eliminating totally unnecessary work and nonproductive employees". Another caller claimed firsthand knowledge of whole departments of workers with no work assignment and an inane department name suggesting activity that does not take place. We have seen reference to such conditions on occasion in our newspapers and periodicals, but apparently reducing our budget by eliminating waste of this kind is without political appeal. Hopefully, in the year 2009, our financial stress will cause much attention being given to such political savings.

29. Can Knowledge Replace Apathy?

What is meant by "knowledge" in this context? It means giving our citizens all available information on both sides of questions being debated by our political representatives and current opinions on both long and short term considerations. In addition, they should have the opportunity to participate in public discussion on important issues. Such participation would not only deepen understanding; it would also obligate politicians to be more objective in their dealings, knowing that a knowledgeable public was out there watching. As mentioned previously, one way of providing a forum for public discussion might be through nonpolitical town hall meetings properly organized for that purpose. Of course, such meetings should provide all available basic information and encourage free thinking. Such an approach requires much development, perhaps along the "Great Books" discussion format. Certainly, rabble-rousing and single-issue-oriented vituperative discussion would not be productive and, as in the "Great Books" discussion format, should not be tolerated.

Up to this time, the attempts to educate the public to vote intelligently have been negligible. This has been observed to a much further extent than our government representatives seems to be aware of. In his book *In Defense of Politics,* Brandon Crick makes the sage observation, "Politics will be richer in the United States when more people come to insist that it is a legitimate aim of education to educate not indoctrinate".

During a recent discussion with a county political party chairman, he revealed that most of the people with whom he dealt in his political job held the attitude, "My mind is made up; don't bother me with the facts". Constructive political discussion is impractical, if not impossible, under such conditions. His response was a follow-up to our expanding the already existent, but almost unknown, political precinct meetings. With prominent leaders of the Moral Majority making such public utterances as "being homosexual is an abomination in the eyes of God" as an example of how inane some people get with their single-issue orientation, perhaps that county political party chairman speaks the truth. If this societal condition represents a total rejection of the concept of applying participative communication to politics, we would have to conclude that our political future is a sorry one indeed.

A study by the Washington Post/Kaiser Foundation reports several sad facts about our qualified voters (voters who are registered to vote). Two-thirds of them cannot name their representatives to Congress and do not know who is the Senate majority leader. Over half do not know which party is more liberal or conservative. The vast majority does not know the length of term of office for most elected officials, and less than 10 percent can name the chief justice of the United States Supreme Court. The county political party chairman who claims that his fellow constituents don't wish to be bothered with the facts certainly seems correct in his assessment. It is easy, therefore, for a dedicated single-issue-oriented campaigner to influence such unenlightened, unthinking people.

The reason for such lack of interest on the part of so many citizens could be anything from disgust with our politicians to frustration caused by the belief that their vote does not matter. It is common to conclude that even if you vote the bad politician out, things will not change.

Although there has been little attempt to educate the people so that they can become knowledgeable voters, there are many programs that, in a small way, try to fill this void. In some high schools, there is what is called a "Citizens Bee", a high school competition based on knowledge of United States history, government, economics, and current events. Because those students who enter such a contest must do considerable reading to be competitive, they become educated as a result. Further, in the process, they are likely to develop the habit of staying informed about civic affairs, a habit which will benefit them throughout their lives. Unfortunately, in areas where such competitions are held, less than one-half of one percent of students enter them, and the areas in which "Citizens Bees" are held are but a very small portion of our country at large.

In Tulsa, Oklahoma, there is an organization called "The Advocates" which is made up of volunteer executives of many organizations who meet regularly to discuss current events that have to do with energy. They train speakers who travel throughout the country trying to educate people on the economics and international politics of the oil and gas industries. It is their observation that ignorance and prejudice about those industries and their importance to our well-being is so prevalent as to result in very bad decision-making by government officials. The negative impact of such bad decisions may cause a severe energy crisis at some point in the future. Perhaps organizations like "The Advocates" duplicated all over the country, would be a means of developing speaker programs dedicated to educating people in civic affairs and politics. Such efforts are, in fact, on-going in the agendas of many nonprofit organizations through which the public becomes more aware of their services. The desired results are greater public awareness of the organization's work, increased membership and volunteerism, and more successful fundraising.

In my observation most adults from any segment of society other than academia are unable to participate in any meaningful discussion having to do with government or our political process. They are either poor listeners, highly prejudiced, uncivil, or insufficiently aware. So long as such is the case, we will continue to trend toward chaos at which point in history democracy will meet its demise à la the Roman Empire. I am optimistic, however, and believe that if we chip away at this seemingly hopeless problem of communication, progress will finally be made, albeit a generation or two from now. How to communicate effectively with the voters is a subject for serious brainstorming.

30. Effective Government Employees

You can rarely do a big job efficiently with employees that are guaranteed job tenure except for gross misconduct, with pay scales that are virtually independent of performance and achievement independent of strong incentives. Most government employees are part of such a system, referred to as the Civil Service. Our Civil Service is organized within a rigid hierarchy that ascribes pay scales and amenities based on job classifications that often have little relationship to the skills required. Retirement and other fringe benefits exceed by far those offered by private industry. Lifetime tenure is virtually assured. Why all this should be so is beyond any explanation except, possibly, that it is the only way to justify the even more exorbitantly generous fringe benefits that often accrue to those who write the rules.

These observations are not meant to demean the efforts of those government employees who are both dedicated and productive. They would also be successful in private industry. However, if ever there was an organization that needed restructuring and/or reengineering, it is our Civil Service! Politics being what they are, however, we are most unlikely to see that happen.

Section VIII

Our Infrastructure

31. Infrastructure

The collapse of a major highway bridge in Minneapolis in August of 2007 is an urgent reminder of the sad condition of thousands of bridges across our country. President Eisenhower led us into the development of a countrywide highway system par excellence. Unfortunately, that system, especially the bridges, has not been well-maintained, and many of the bridges cannot pass safety inspection today. Further, the growth of automobile traffic loads suggests that major bridges would be designed today with more stringent engineering requirements than was the case back then. It behooves us to address this problem hastily before bridge failures like that in Minneapolis result in further loss of life. Unfortunately, our huge indebtedness deters us from doing so in a businesslike manner. Thus, we will probably address this problem largely by responding only to emergencies – as too often is the case.

The problem with bridges is symptomatic of our entire infrastructure – not only the portions our federal government is responsible for, but also roads and bridges that states and cities are responsible for. In the case of local and interstate roads, both severe heat and cold, particularly ice, often leave surface damage that slows traffic, sometimes causes accidents, and causes vehicular damage due to constant vibration. It seems that we are financially limited in our ability to take care of such problems in a timely manner.

Many highway improvements geared toward preventing accidents have been made, however. Highway engineers have not been complacent. These changes include the following:

- Surface grooving to make water run off more rapidly, thereby minimizing vehicle water-planing and accidents that may result
- Improved guardrails that minimize vehicle damage and severe accidents caused by running off the road
- Use of barrel formations to absorb vehicle shock when cars stray from the highway
- Serrated surfaces that produce vibration and perceptible noise when vehicles stray from a normal path, perhaps due to driver drowsiness
- Improved highway on/off ramps
- Sturdy highway median barriers to prevent cars from straying into opposing traffic

The foregoing changes are gradually being implemented – but ever so slowly. There are locks and dams on the upper Mississippi River that are eighty years old, long past the time of needing major repair or replacement. The amount of commercial traffic that travels the Mississippi is huge. Similarly, harbors, airports, river levees, and electrical distribution systems are all suffering from neglect. The failure of levees in New Orleans is an example, and because those levees were replaced or repaired to a serviceable standard that is little better than they were before Katrina, there is real worry that they would again fail if subjected to another Katrina-class hurricane. In my previous career, I related with many geologists who said that the path of the Mississippi through New Orleans is gradually changing and our efforts to outwit nature there are likely to fail in the long term. If so, that is another catastrophe waiting to happen that would inundate much of New Orleans.

Part Two

Can We Replace Social Disorder with Social Harmony?

Steering the Maturation of Humankind with the Aid of an Historical Crystal Ball

Introduction

Stewart Brand, publisher of *The Whole Earth Catalog,* is considered by many critics to be a typical iconoclast, but it might be more accurate to describe him as a consummate freethinker. Because of that ability, he has been an invited participant in many esoteric discussions at the Santa Fe Institute. He said in a television interview on March 2nd, 2004 that because mind-boggling change is ever-present, focusing on the avoidance of major blunders yields better results than focusing only on the big win. He was quick to point out that this involves finding strategies that will work reasonably well in every scenario that can be imagined. It involves applying freethinking from an historical view-point; that is, a thinking process in which, from an imag-ined scenario of the future, you look back at the present to evaluate what is happening now and how we can ben-eficially influence trends and change. This takes talented and strategic imagination; it is more than mere forecasting. Most often, in fact, we cannot forecast accurately. We can, however, envision possible future scenarios and evaluate them for both desirability and possible responses. This process is referred to here as using "an historical crystal ball and could be used as a valuable planning tool by or-ganizations involved in long range planning.

32. Mission Statements Would Help

In a well-run business, modern management techniques require a mission statement, job descriptions, and an answer to the question, "What is our business?" Inculcating such steps into the political arena would not be easy and would meet with almost impossible resistance. But applying them to the degree possible could eliminate many useless jobs that now account for much waste. Establishing job descriptions with expectations for results could result in improved focus and efficiency. With regard to the question "What is our business?", many public servants lack definitions of the responsibilities of their departments, limitations that apply, or the obligation to communicate and cooperate with other departments, committees or branches of government.

33. Management in Politics

The mores and worldliness of peoples everywhere change over time, hopefully in a constructive manner - making for a better world. As Tom Friedman says in his book *The World is Flat*, "each century, as we push out the frontiers of human knowledge, work at every level becomes more complex, requiring more pattern recognition and problem solving". Thus far, we have been able to adapt. Yes, we may be guilty of going forward three steps and then regressing two, but from a historical viewpoint if we are improving in terms of interpersonal relationships, scientific accomplishment, education, health, and overall living standards, I refer to that as "The Maturation of Humankind".

It is not difficult to find evidence of mismanagement of our country and our world which certainly would not contribute positively to the maturation of humankind. Although awareness of this can and does cause much consternation for the serious-minded person, it does not produce answers to the question, "How can we improve things?" In this topic, revisions are proposed in our approach to managing change which, if implemented, could very much enhance progress. Even when mistakes are made, with the use of a participative approach, understanding rather than resentment and divisiveness, will prevail. Recall the old adage, "Tell me and I may forget; show me and I may remember; involve me and I will understand". Further, properly prepared responses to deviations from the original plan should permit getting back on course, or an acceptable revised course, within a reasonable time.

In applying professional management techniques to business enterprises, it is common to go through an exercise called a SWOT list which is a review of strengths, weaknesses, opportunities and threats. In reflecting on the material covered by sections I through VIII, we see considerable reference to weaknesses in our society and our attempts to beneficially influence a variety of vicissitudes impacting us. In those topics, many trends toward chaos are clearly evident, but the need to control and reverse such trends has not yet become sufficiently emergency-like in character to reach beyond that unstable fence called politics.

As is true in business management, an in-depth review of a SWOT list, although a very useful exercise, has long-term value only if the data generated is applied in a pragmatic manner. Doing so with socioeconomic issues, such as reducing poverty, can often provoke political conflict but could be aided by the following:

- Objectives must be long-term, and they must allow time for a meaningful future to be realized.
- Objectives must be achievable at affordable cost.
- The required planning must minimize "politics". It must involve the use of think tanks or planning groups capable of creating likely scenarios of the future (the Historical Crystal Ball).

- The planning must be participative, provide open access to all available data and solicit broad input from all who may be affected by the results of the plan.
- The plan must provide for monitoring.
- The plan must provide responses to deviations. Rather than merely being considered a group of conclusions, it is a process that permits coping with uncertainty and changing conditions.
- Each legislator must be permitted to think and vote freely without pressure applied by legislative "whips" urging conformance to the will of the majority in the party.

There should be no exceptions to the foregoing tenets without good reason. The usual management of the legislative process to permit arriving at preconceived opinions, including in-depth interviewing of only those people who hold a particular opinion, must be stopped. To inculcate the public and all politicians with such attitudes requires that they first be convinced that such an approach will improve the quality of life for all of us. At the very least, it can prevent a social apocalypse in our future. Deciding which party gets the credit should be given a backseat to the long-range good for society.

Many things in government that might have been considered too liberal a hundred years ago such as Medicare and Social Security are now considered necessary, oftentimes even conservative With the realization that history changes mores and public need, it would be well, in the interest of long-term thinking, to eliminate the political terms "liberal" and "conservative" when referring to legislation. Too often, in today's political climate, we elect a person to political office merely because he or she is a liberal or a conservative. We should elect a person because he or she is capable of thinking and voting in the long-term interest of the country, which requires intelligence, dedication, and the desire to do right even when it does not please the most voters or political supporters. That a Republican party is made up of members or supporters with more conservative leanings than those who make up a party of Democrats is fine, and the country probably benefits from the rivalry. But, too often, total allegiance to "the team", even to the point of voting contrary to one's individual logic, is apt to have a long-term negative impact.

In business, were we to spend huge sums of money to be sure that a potential manager would think exactly as the CEO thinks, very little would be accomplished. No one is perfect, and if a political candidate or appointee does not fit the mold of any group empowered to stand in that person's way, it only takes money to investigate deeply enough to find some irrelevant reason for that person to be rejected. Relevant reasons for rejection, in this context, should apply only to conduct that reflects inability to do the job. Of course, integrity toward the office and the voting constituents should be mandatory.

34. Religion

Religion is and often has been a source of serious harm to humankind, including much loss of life. Throughout history, many religions have had sects or segments that believed in and practiced sadistic cruelty and murder in the furtherance of what they believed was the desire of their god. In so doing, they abandon even the slightest regard for human dignity. It is such thinking that has spawned pogroms, jihads, crusades, the Holocaust, and many other mass demonstrations of man's inhumanity to man. A recently observed bumper sticker read, "I'm for separation of church and hate".

Because religion can, and in our country does, have a deep and positive influence on our lives, we might benefit from it more were we to study the evolution of religion. Such a study might start with the gradual migration of early humankind from northeastern Africa to most parts of the world–a migration that occurred very slowly, over centuries. Anthropologists indicate that earliest humankind did not have verbal communicative skills as we now know them. Verbal communication, they say, was by the use of oral sounds referred to as "clicks". Multiple clicks and groupings of clicks were used in a manner that conveyed meanings as we now use words. Even today, clicks are an important part of the language among several tribes in remote parts of Africa. Were you to encounter these tribes, perhaps while on an adventurous trek, you would usually find them responding to you with a pleasant demeanor. Perhaps you could conclude that because they are not yet truly integrated into our modern civilization they have not yet developed a predilection to incivility, greed, or a "know-it-all" attitude.

Because tribes usually were very distant from one another, communication between tribes was a rarity. In relatively recent history, our American Indians still used smoke signals, although as they demonstrated in their help to our military during the Second World War, they have had verbal skills for centuries. Verbal communication, as we now know it, evolved over hundreds of years.

In virtually every migrating tribe we can assume that there were those who dwelled on the basic questions about the existence of humankind. Such wondering is natural. Probably from such thinking came the origins of religion, but the lack of communication between tribes permitted each to arrive at different conclusions. There are no actual records on which to base that thinking, but historically, that may very well be the reason we have so many religions. In each case, however, initial thinking had to include certain assumptions.

Many years ago I participated in a very small religious study group that enjoyed the cooperation of several clergymen. One began with the statement, "In my religion we start out with certain assumptions which are not up for discussion". That admission by a highly respected ordained clergyman truly impressed our group. Here was a statement by a learned clergyman which really admitted that we believe in an almighty by choice not through actual knowledge. It seemed to us that his statement derived from his studies at the divinity school where he earned his ordination. Because he did not have to worry about being quoted by anyone in our group, his candor exceeded by far that which he might have used with his parishioners-at-large. To do so with them probably would have greatly reduced his ability to be of positive influence. If you randomly pose the statement to individuals, "The concept of God derives from man, and all biblical writings were written by man", you will get virtually 100 percent agreement. I have posed that statement well over 300 times, and agreement has been the only response I have had until one recent exception. That lone exception was from a lady who was a devotee of an evangelical minister who had her mesmerized with the conclusion that "the Book" was her only source of "truth". She refused to give any thought to the fact that her "Book" was written by man. You will observe that most people have to pause and think about the statement's thrust before voicing their agreement. That is because they have not been impacted previously by such a statement which, at first, seems to conflict with their beliefs.

To the degree that we agree, then, that assumptions had to be made in the origins of any religion, each of us can ask the question of a member of any other church, "Do you consider your assumptions better than mine, or ours, or merely different?"

Very few people initiate their religious philosophy with any consideration of assumptions. Rather, most begin with beliefs that include a belief in God, a belief in their Bible being divinely inspired and, in the case of many Christians, in the divinity of Jesus Christ as the Son of God. These beliefs can, and often do, become very fervent. The result is that they devoutly spend a great deal of time in church activities and Bible study. To the degree that religion is often a source of inner peace for them, it can be a most positive factor in their lives.

Often these beliefs deepen with time and finally dwell in the realm of what I refer to as "spiritual conviction" and assume an aura of certainty. Perhaps it is that certainty that limits understanding of people who think differently. We should, at least subconsciously, remember the involvement of assumptions to prevent such overreaction and lack of understanding. You might think that a profound belief in an Almighty should make one feel somewhat humble–not entirely sure of God's intentions for us mortals – but, alas, such is not the case.

Usually, our religious affiliation is that of our parents. Over time we become imbued with a sense of belonging and may derive much psychological comfort from that affiliation. A charismatic clergyperson often enhances the value system of parishioners, who also may be enriched by their togetherness in many ways. These religious attributes are fine unless presented in a very manipulative, controlling manner, as evangelical-type churches are prone to do with the admonishment: "Those who profess religious beliefs different from ours are infidels and are barred from acceptance into heaven". How can thinking people obediently conform to such abasement of others when even the concept of heaven derives from the thinking of man?

Many charismatic ministers succeed in mesmerizing their "flocks" with their preferred religious dogma. Too often, they neglect to teach the reasons why the adoption and practice of basic goodness (or, if you prefer, righteous-ness) in our lives is of great long-term benefit to us all. Merely referring to the Golden Rule or the Ten Command-ments, even with frequency, doesn't quite serve to make us righteous.

We all ask how a truly righteous person can believe in stoning another human to death for violating the tenets of a church or how the intentional killing of totally inno-cent fellow humans can be justified. With Adolph Hitler castigated by history for having been responsible for the slaughter of millions of people, you would think that such abhorrent behavior, often referred to as "ethnic cleansing", could no longer exist. Unfortunately, it still exists in the year 2008 and is responsible for the deaths of thousands of innocent people. The United Nations Refugee Agency reports that over 240,000 people have lost their lives in Darfur as of this writing. Such complete abandonment of the Golden Rule is a disgrace to humankind. How can peo-ple possibly believe that such actions are sanctioned by God? And whereas many nations were harshly criticized for not having stopped Hitler early on, there is very little controlling action of consequence by the nations at large against what has been happening in Darfur.

This discussion is appropriate herein because religion has intertwined itself in our politics in a manner not in sym-pathy with the divine thoughts on which any religion is based. Religion has become too businesslike, to the point at which even the highly regarded Reverend Jerry Falwell found it necessary to enroll in a management course given by the American Management Association. Clergymen too often are more interested in the size of their church's membership and budget growth than in their spiritual obligations to their congregation.

It should be unlawful, or at least unethical, to even suggest to church members whom they should vote for, even if the reason for doing seems to be ethically based and therefore nonpolitical. Such advice to parishioners is certainly political and is prohibited by law. So far, the legal limitations required for tax-exempt status do not quite keep churches free of politics. The powerful political influence of what has become known as the "Religious Right" may or may not be harmful in the long term, but certainly it prevents, in many ways, the true and thoughtful opinions of a thinking voting public and is contrary to the principle of "separation of church and state". It has been reported that former President George W. Bush, who is regarded as a "Born Again Christian", made many of his leadership decisions based on his personal "communications" with God. His percentage of good decisions was pretty low, as reflected in recent polls that rated his approval by the public lower than 30 percent. Political decisions should be made only after due consideration of available facts and projection of results, both long and short term. Sometimes, as in business, it would be appropriate to set benchmarks to evaluate effectiveness and the possible need for subsequent amendment or change.

Many years ago the poem "Abou Ben Adhem", by James Henry Hunt, was so well regarded as to be a required subject for memorization in many public schools. Its basic philosophy is very worthwhile.

Abou Ben Adhem
Abou Ben Adhem (may his tribe increase!)
Awoke one night from a deep dream of peace,
And saw, within the moonlight in his room,
Making it rich, and like a lily in bloom,
An Angel writing in a book of gold.
Exceeding peace had made Ben Adhem bold,
And to the Presence in the room he said,
"What writest thou?" The Vision raised its head,
And with a look made of all sweet accord
Answered, "The names of those who love the Lord."
"And is mine one?" said Abou. "Nay, not so,"
Replied the angel. Abou spoke more low,
But cheerily still, and said, "I pray thee, then,
Write me as one that loves his fellow-men."
The Angel wrote, and vanished. The next night
It came again with a great wakening light,
And showed the names whom God had blessed,
And lo! Ben Adhem's name led all the rest.

Helen Keller was born blind and deaf but became a highly respected motivational speaker. She was belligerently resistant to education in her early childhood years, but as an adult she became avidly thirsty for knowledge. She is quoted as having said, "I seek not the peace which passeth understanding. I seek understanding which bringeth peace". She may or may not have said that in a religious context, but the last portion of the quotation certainly is germane in this religious commentary. Some religions or religious groups are overtly intolerant with regard to others. Some are tolerant—an abhorrent word that by definition can include tolerance of unpleasant things or thinking. Some are understanding, which implies knowledge of, and even advocating love and compassion for one's fellow man. If all churchgoers were to strongly advocate, as one of the precepts sanctioned by the Almighty, the love of one's fellow man we would have a much better world! Until all major religions and religious groups teach, practice, and believe in such understanding, religion will continue, at times, to bridge the gap between concept and chaos!

35. An Historical Crystal Ball

Concepts for the improvement of humankind, a business, or the environment, even when accompanied by what would be considered exquisite conventional (linear) planning, cannot be left unattended to mature with only conventional implementation procedures. The prevalence of random unpredictable influences will almost always destroy the plan in a chaotic manner. Dependable long-range policies cannot be made based merely on logic and scientific facts. After such statements, are we to assume that chaos is inevitable and beyond hope? Indeed not!

None of us has an historical crystal ball to tell precisely how the changes we experience today will impact our society from an historical viewpoint. That also is true of almost all of the long-range planning done by business or government. Nonetheless, businesses and many branches of government should benefit from their involvement in long-range strategic planning.

The suggested use of an "historical crystal ball", although rare, is a planning technique used by a few larger corporations, such as Royal Dutch Shell. Some think tanks also use this type of planning approach. It requires a leader and participants capable of long-range conceptualizing.

Because the future usually fails to materialize precisely as a planning team envisions, progress must be monitored against pre-established benchmarks. As deviation from expectation is observed, the plan must be revised to account for new conditions. In this manner, planning can become responsive to change. Such deviation can be the result of both present and evolving influences that are often unpredictable, and sometimes illogical; and, because the deviation is rarely of the type that can be referred to as "linear", in that it happens too slowly, too rapidly, or in a manner that had previously been considered unlikely, the planning process proposed herein is referred to as "non-linear planning".

Changes of the type referred to in topics I through VIII are much more complex than those which typically impact businesses, and planning for and responding to them requires a broad spectrum of expertise. The types of organizations we refer to as "think tanks" can and should be used to provide a vision, or scenario, of the future to which planning teams can respond on each of those topics. A vision of the future, in this context, must include not only predicting the long-term impacts of on-going trends but also envisioning the impact of remote, but possible, influences. Such thinking can serve us well as an "historical crystal ball" if we keep that vision up to date by reviewing it often and revising it as necessary. It should be considered an ongoing process, and it must be objective.

This sort of long-range planning does not seem to take place in the realm of politics. For that reason, it may be useful to go through an example. Suppose we theoretically apply this approach to a serious problem from which we now suffer: crime. The think tanks would make a study of crime from the following vantage points:

1. The history of crime in America
    a. Numerical trends
    b. Types of crime and their prevalence
    c. Psychological and economic profiles of criminals
2. Deterrents that have been and are being used
3. Types of punishment
4. Effectiveness of law and law enforcement
5. Sociological causes for criminal behavior
6. The effect of education and environment on criminal behavior
7. A vision of the future if trends that are now prevalent continue
8. The potential positive results of legalizing marijuana. In some countries, it has been found that legalizing marijuana has reduced serious crime caused by drug lords. This should be studied.

The planning teams would then discuss these studies and begin to organize their thinking in the following way:

1. What is the best way to protect society from various types of criminals when we know that we cannot change anyone in the short term?
    a. Habitual adult criminals
    b. First-time adult criminals
    c. Crime by children
    d. Terrorists
    e. Crime associated with mental illness
2. What potential exists for the use of drugs and/or surgical procedures for people with identifiable criminal traits, some of which may prove to be of genetic

origin? Much progress has already been made in this area but the findings are not being used largely because of lack of understanding and political restraints.

3. What can be done to rehabilitate criminals?
   a. Review past rehabilitation efforts
   b. Establish a plan for pervasively applying throughout our prison systems those rehabilitation efforts that have been effective
   c. Modify our pardon and parole systems to maximize effectiveness
4. What can be done to eliminate poor parenting and poor home environment which inadvertently foster criminal behavior to a great degree?
5. How we can change our educational system to instill moral values and self-discipline and teach that crime does not pay and is degrading to the quality of life for everyone?
   a. Approaches for educating children and adults
   b. Using proven approaches of the military-like training

When considering the above scenario, no individual would have sufficient expertise to do such planning. It truly takes a planning team or teams.

It would next be necessary to develop a plan to effectively protect society soon after implementation, and to gradually reduce crime by beneficially influencing parenting and psychological environment. Goals and benchmarks of progress would be set and monitored. At each benchmark, the plan would be reviewed and revised as necessary. If this sounds simplistic, such would not be the case. It would prove to be an arduous process that would have to begin with nonpartisan commitment by government and followed by the selection of multiple think tanks and planning groups. The proposed plan would be submitted back to the think tanks for long-range evaluation. The initial cost would be huge, but the long-term savings would be vastly greater when the present overall cost of crime is considered.

The public would have to be educated on the entire plan so that they would understand it well. This does not mean that the plan should be sold to them as politicians are wont to do. Government will work much more effectively if we exhibit trust in our citizenry by giving them the necessary tools, in this case knowledge, and let them think for themselves. It is time we stopped swaying them with half truths, propaganda, and inane Congressional questionnaires wastefully mailed to constituents. It is time to stop expecting them to agree with one political side or the other and, instead, ask them to reason for the benefit of society. Those most capable of clear thinking will uplift those who arrive at logical conclusions more slowly. If they could be shown that with short-term sacrifice (cost), there would be decidedly long-term payback, I like to believe that people will respond intelligently.

Several recent observations are deserving of mention herein, since they pertain importantly to the problem of crime in America: Dr. Sheldon Hackney, former president of the University of Pennsylvania, is responsible for an idea called "National Conversation", which the National Endowment for the Humanities has funded with over $4 million.

That program engages thousands of people in structured discussions about what it means to be an American. Examples of this effort are: (1) a grant of almost $400,000 to the American Library Association to support one hundred conversational groups in twenty states on American values, (2) a grant to Tufts University for a series of discussions centered on the subject "The immigrant experience", and (3) a series of discussions held in Alaska on the subject "How Americans are faring in Alaska, our country's last frontier". As of this writing, it appears likely that the latter program may suffer because of lack of funding.

Dr. Hackney's idea certainly has merit, but because it provides neither participation nor understanding by the electorate it fails to specifically educate about our political process. Certainly, the conversations he envisions are healthy in that they improve understanding among those who participate.

An article in *The Wall Street Journal* of August 3, 1994, entitled "Crime Prevention - the Criminals' View" not only provides enlightening insight into the problem of crime; it also indicates that many criminals would be happy to help in a long-range effort to reduce crime.

36. Non-linear Planning

Two violinists can play the same composition, emitting identical notes and having like tonal quality, and one will sound better than, or different from, the other. When asked why this is so, the famous violinist Isaac Stern replied, "The difference is in the intervals between the notes". He may have intended his response to be facetious, but he spoke the truth even if his answer is not complete. Given an intended interval between two notes of thirty milliseconds, for example, one violinist might dwell on the first note for twelve milliseconds and, in staccato fashion, provide a mere five millisecond interval before starting the second note. Another violinist might dwell a few milliseconds on note one and then, without a noticeable interval, phase into note two.

Stern, in responding to a non-performer, did not give a detailed answer. The tonal quality produced by a violin also depends on the quality of the violin, the physical character of the violinist's fingertips, and myriad other variables. The subjective interpretation of the performer also influences the rendition considerably. Perhaps Stern was grouping all these factors into his phrase "the intervals between the notes".

Imagine, then, how varied the sound from a symphony orchestra can be, largely controlled by the interpretation of the conductor who causes the individual instruments and groups of instruments to play with varying degrees of relative intensity, tremolo, or tempo, just to name some his or her possible influences.

We constantly try to improve the direction, intensity, and long-range impact that ever-present change may have on the social welfare of humankind or on our environment, including the continuing existence of the world's many plant and animal species. Our attempts to do so would have greater chance of success if orchestrated as in the realm of music. Such orchestration would be infinitely more complex than in the example of symphonic music. The time under consideration can be centuries, not minutes. The random influences to be considered are huge in number, not merely several dozen instruments.

Because, from an historical view, such planning and plan execution are so prone to chaos, "orchestration" must be much different in character. Personal goals held by those involved must be subordinated to long-range scenarios conceived in the broad-based interest of the people. In fact, such thinking is so different from normal planning techniques as to require a new vocabulary. It probably requires three or four highly qualified think tanks that would be totally free of political or religious prejudice. This does not mean that they must be antireligious or anti-political.

In mathematics, change that is linear is predictable, whereas change that is not linear usually requires the use of calculus for problem solving. Even calculus cannot be used to solve problems that are subject to randomness, as is the case with weather forecasting.

Thus far, most solutions for long-range social problems that have emanated from so-called "think tanks" also have proven to be ineffective, and the clock keeps ticking on our way to world ecological and social chaos. This is not surprising, considering that most such problems are so complex as to defy the use of computer models to study the manner in which they usually evolve from concept to chaos. They really are beyond typical planning to all except those who assume they have all the answers. In some attempts to use high powered computers to predict the future, huge banks of historical data have been employed, using what is called neural-network technology, with little success. When applied to the stock market, such technology has proven to be worthless in picking long-term trends.

One ray of hope lies in the organizational concept of the Santa Fe Institute, a multi-disciplined group of scientists who meet to discuss our more serious world problems. On the positive side, they use an approach in which the individuals involved interrelate in a manner which recognizes that the more deeply scientists study our serious problems, the more the branches of science overlap, resulting in their definitions becoming blurred. The biologist learns that he depends on mathematics, the environmentalist must use chemistry, the astrophysicist depends on conventional physics, etc. Such understanding fosters better progress through team effort.

Encouraging each individual scientist to participate fully in the work of the group requires a director who is sensitive to the frequent preference of research personnel for working alone and protecting his or her turf. The director subtly encourages conscientious application, blending, and timing of the special expertise each possesses and the appreciation that each will enrich his or her special expertise through understanding the different perspectives of the others. On the negative side, the work of the Santa Fe Institute and that of many other such think tanks that come to mind has limited financial support, and that which they do have often requires attention to specified projects. There is very limited public awareness of the work they are doing, and in most instances, each research group is unaware of what other groups are doing. There is very little cross- fertilization to minimize duplication and provide synergism.

An article in the July 3, 1995 issue of *Business Week* listed eight organizations referred to as Washington's brain trusts. Their average 1994 revenues amounted to over twelve million dollars, indicating that they are fairly large organizations. The article also noted political attitudes for which each was known, running from conservative through libertarian to liberal. A true think tank, capable of recommending solutions for social problems that result from non-linear planning, should not have political leanings or prejudicial attitudes even though, as individuals, we all have prejudices. It seems inappropriate that our politicians are permitted to spend our dollars so profusely in their quest for prejudiced answers. They can think that way, without help, at a much lower cost.

Many think tanks are able to survive handsomely because of substantial endowment. The Brookings Institute has an endowment of over $150 million, and there are others that have endowments at least that large. Whether these endowment monies carry with them any long-term thought-confining obligations is unknown, but monies are frequently offered them for research that would support specified conclusions. Also, many big givers to political parties are frustrated by the legal limitations that apply to such giving. They sometimes circumvent limitations by giving, without legal constraints, to a think tank utilized by their chosen political party. Yes, most employees of think tanks usually have superior intellectual capacity, and sometimes are sources of key government appointees. However, changes need to be made to improve their objectivity. As Rex Stout once said, "There are two kinds of statistics, the kind you look up and the kind you make up". Using a consulting organization that has a built-in bias, as politicians are prone to do, is akin to Rex Stout's reference to statistics of "the kind you make up".

We have all heard variations of the expression, "Things will have to get a lot worse before we will be motivated to make them better". As of the moment, that expression seems to apply, but we better not wait too long!

Section X

In Conclusion

Conclusions

In this text there is much criticism of our elected officials and their work. Quoting from a Rasmussen Report, "Just 12% say Congress doing a good or excellent job. 54% say Congress doing poor job". I have read a yet unpublished book by a local would-be comedian, who would prefer to remain anonymous, in which he has referred to "con" being the opposite of "pro" and applied that reference to Congress as the opposite of progress. Our elected members of congress are, however, deserving of understanding. Usually a member of Congress has little clout or influence during the first year or early years in office. If reelection is desired, he or she must spend considerable time and energy during the last year or years in office campaigning. Certainly this is true if the desire to be of influence is present, because appointments to influential committees, largely earned by length of service, are virtual requirements for being effective. Then we make it necessary for the candidate to raise huge amounts of money that are accompanied by deep obligation to the donors, many of whom seek influence. Correcting this system should have high priority. A candidate should not have to spend so much time soliciting campaign funds and certainly should not have to compromise his or her sense of duty. In his 2007 campaign efforts, then Senator Barack Obama successfully solicited small contributions from large numbers of voters who would not be classified as rich. Although that, in itself, may or may not have been a viable factor in his political future, it does illustrate that a presidential candidate can run for office without having to depend on large contributions.

Another perspective that a politician should adopt as part of a working modus operandi has to do with the sense of financial well-being and future security. Elected officials are provided with generous retirement funds and paid medical care. There supposedly are also numerous "perks" which, for many, include the personal assumption of unused campaign funds after retirement. Although such remaining unused funds can be substantial, it is my understanding that they must be used for charitable causes only. They are not intended for personal use, although personal benefit may result from the payment of any charitable pledges made that formerly had to be paid with personal funds. If these conditions are real, there should be no excuse for seeking further riches while in office that have even the least potential of influencing decision making. There should be no possibility that people or organizations will reward you for your political activity, either while in office or after you retire from office. Not to subscribe to such principles would be indicative of greed. For the rare case of a person retired from any national elected office being in financial need, perhaps there should be an endowed fund to draw on. Such principles should permit a politician to devote his or her conscientious efforts to the job without ever having to resort to self-serving actions.

In the section of this book entitled "Religion" is a quote from Helen Keller. That quote was found, of all places, as a cryptoquote in a local newspaper. In my semi-retirement

I find much enjoyment and relaxation in working crypto-quotes and crossword puzzles. Another recent crypto-quote, when completed, read, "If you want to learn a lot about a subject, try writing a book about it". I've forgotten the name of the person quoted, but the writing of this book has validated, for me, that quotation. I had been aware that the number of government agencies is large, but in the course of composing this book I have learned that my previous awareness was lacking considerably. Were you to list the acronyms assigned to these agencies (usually expressed in three or four letters) in normal print size, it might be too long to fit a full-length newspaper column. It has been claimed by former government employees (see topic 28, *We the People as Employers and Managers*) that there are more than a few agencies which no longer have a useful function due to changes that have evolved since their formation; further, many do not have well-defined goals. The results are gross inefficiency and monetary waste. Even worse is the lack of interdepartmental cooperation, as was the case with the almost zero interaction level between the CIA and the FBI before the 9/11 debacle. As government gets increasingly complex, perhaps an overseer of interdepartmental coordination needs to be elevated to cabinet status.

Now that Barack Obama is our president, it is time to forget why one political party may be better than the other and realize that such suppositions are usually based on erroneous short-term thinking. It is more important than ever for us to come together and understand the dire financial circumstances we now are in. As in all such conditions, were we talking about a business, there are only the usual changes that can possibly solve the problem: reduce expenditures, increase income, or a combination of both. In topic 27 ("Is the United States Broke Financially?") several methods for reducing our annual budget are listed, and there are probably many more. All of these need to be investigated, but as has been pointed out, implementing them may cause considerable upset and even necessary changes in our lifestyle. Therefore, our new president has a big job convincing the public of such needs and asking for our patriotic cooperation. When we think of the great communicators among our presidents, the names Lincoln, Roosevelt, Kennedy, and Reagan come to mind. Barack Obama seems to be regarded as a potential member of that group. If so, he may prove to be the right man at the right time.

In his speech to Congress on February 24th, 2009 President Obama outlined a broad agenda for reform in health care, energy, education, taxation and several other facets of government. He seemed to "touch all the bases" in a very bold manner accompanied by an air of confidence in our ability to overcome almost insurmountable problems. His speech reflected the long term approach expressed in his book *Audacity of Hope*. I can only assume that he has an accurate overall realization of how severe our national indebtedness is, as outlined in Topic 25 "Our Withering Democracy". My worry has to do with the previous lack of accuracy by Congress and former administration officials when talking about balancing our budget. That he fully appreciates the severity of our budgetary problems but does not allude to it may be because doing so could have negative psychological implications. That would be understandable, but it would be immensely reassuring to know how all the changes and plans he has in mind will ultimately lead to a balanced budget. Only by reaching a point where federal income exceeds budgeted expenditures can we hope to reduce our indebtedness and as suggested in Topic 25 that may require a change in our lifestyle and mores. A plan to reach and finally exceed a balanced budget would most likely have a persuasive impact on the political far right.

His plan to use an appreciable portion of the recently approved Stimulus Package as a means to create jobs by repairing our infrastructure is reminiscent of the Works Project Administration created by Franklin Roosevelt in the 1930s which was not only a big success but also left us with so many benefits that we still enjoy.

He referred to changes in taxation which will certainly benefit the middle class but ultimately will increase taxes on the wealthy when some of their tax reductions initiated under the George W. Bush administration expire. People who may then suffer increased taxation point out that they are now paying almost 80 percent of our total taxes and after 2011, they could be paying almost 90 percent of our total taxes according to a recent report I heard on CNN. That may be true, but to control our financial destiny and prevent excessive concentration of wealth, it may be justified – even necessary.

The intransigence of the Congressional Republicans in failing to respond to President Obama's attempts to engender a team approach toward solving our problems is disappointing. Such an attitude could very easily evoke ire on the part of the President, but fortunately he seems to be taking it in stride and will continue to seek their co-operation and constructive criticism. So far, he appears to be a superior communicator. I hope history will deem him a good leader.

And last, but not least: I am inherently an optimist and occasionally have indicated idealism in this book. If the vast majority of people believe that idealism too often is impractical and a mere expression of hopeless platitudes, the World will continue on a downward chaotic path as Al Gore says with regard to our environment and global warming.

Most of us have experienced inner pleasure from observing a young child's happiness resulting from humor or kindness we have extended. When we learn to derive that kind of inner pleasure from expressing consideration for our fellow humans (righteousness, if you will), the many ills discussed herein may be on the mend. This is not so difficult to do if we just think such good thoughts when extending help to a friend, charity to one in need, civility to a stranger, or when we contribute talent to a worthy cause. The list is potentially endless and the inner pleasure very self-rewarding.

Made in the USA